HOUSE CONVERSION
AND RENEWAL

HOUSE CONVERSION AND RENEWAL

PETER COLLYMORE

The Architectural Press Limited

This book is dedicated to owners, architects, surveyors, local authority administrators and inspectors, building contractors, their sub-contractors and suppliers and all others involved in the conversion and extension of houses with the hope that it will help bring their endeavours to a satisfactory conclusion.

examples redrawn by Derek Taylor

Photographic Acknowledgements

Figures refer to pages in which illustrations occur

Antoine Raffoul: 133–35; *Building Research Establishment*: 65–72; *Brecht-Einzig*: 125–28, 153–55; *Castle Park Dean & Hook*: 176; *Fielden & Mawson*: 164–65; *Ideal Home*: 140–43; *John Dewar Studios*: 157; *Keith Gibson*: viii, 10, 30, 118–22, 160–63, 172–75; *Manchester Guardian*: 179–82; *Michael Wickham*: 95–98; *John Wyatt/Scottish Field*: 156–57; *W. Toomey*: 100–03, 108–17, 129–32, 137–39, 144–51, 169–71; *Jo Reid*: 104–05, 107; *Lisa Nobbs*: 177–78; *David Jenkins*: 165 lower.

First published 1975 by The Architectural Press Ltd: London

Reprinted 1976
Reprinted 1977

© Peter Collymore 1975
ISBN: 0 85139 002 1

Filmset and printed in Great Britain by BAS Printers Limited, Over Wallop, Hampshire

Contents

Preface

In writing this book I had in mind not only architects or surveyors with some experience but those perhaps tackling a conversion contract for the first time. It is intended to help prevent the professional falling into the Slough of Despond, but, if he does, to show him the stepping stones to dry land.

However, I hope that not only professionals may find the book useful and of interest. To anyone reading it, it must become obvious what a complicated and regulated affair house conversion is. If the owner can appreciate what his professional adviser or builder is up against, it will help understanding between all sides.

If there is knowledge of when and where the regulations are likely to impinge on the design and supervision of a conversion contract, then success is more likely to be achieved and the building operation can be finished at the expected time for a reasonable price.

Awareness of the constraints will give the architect or surveyor confidence when designing the work and enable him to spend more time and energy on what really matters, the architecture.

Introduction

The regeneration, extension and alteration of existing buildings is part of the history of architecture as well as providing a record of social change.

As children, probably the first plan of a building we ever set eyes on is of the local parish church or cathedral. The civic pride of one's parents, let alone religious reasons, may have taken us there at an early age. We puzzled on the plan, likely to be a patchwork of different shadings representing perhaps the Saxon, EE, 'perp', building periods which more often than not have ended in a homogeneity of architecture, although separated by many years.

Each phase tells us about the advances in engineering, use of materials and their availability, changes in liturgy and the social development of the society using the building as well, of course, as the architectural theories developing contemporaneously with all those factors.

As with the houses of God, so it is with those of the citizens.

The towns and cities we live in are a testimony to their development, their periods of affluence and decay, of the materials available for building them and the special skills of the inhabitants. Individual houses are governed by the same factors.

Haddon Hall, Derbyshire. Built, extended and altered many times between 1070 and 1624, Haddon Hall reflects the changes in the fortunes and aspirations of its owners over that time.

The illustration of the plan of Haddon Hall, Derbyshire, shows the various phases of extension spread over many years which have gone to make a conglomerate building of great interest.

Although this is a rather grand example of a building which has developed

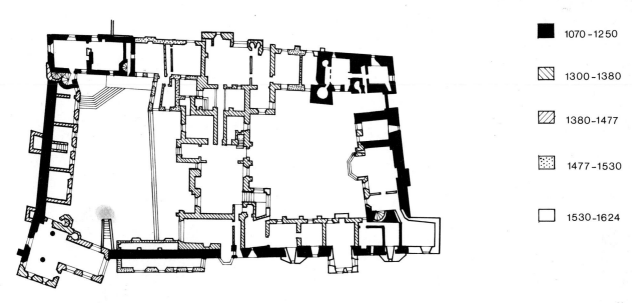

■ 1070-1250

◩ 1300-1380

▨ 1380-1477

▦ 1477-1530

☐ 1530-1624

The first sight may be daunting.

and expanded, it is just one facet of the continuing alteration and renewal process of buildings and towns.

As the population increases so does the demand for dwellings and for larger spaces to live in. One also has to take into account that the preceding eras of house building, notably the 19th-century urbanisation of the industrial revolution, have left us with houses which we must demolish and replace or renovate and make more suitable as well as healthier to live in.

However, a healthy society should develop an architecture which is innovatory, satisfying and suitable to its needs for its new buildings which will be inherited and appreciated by the future inhabitants. Conservation, renovation and alteration is all very well for the right buildings but a nation which lives in nothing but the patched up left-overs from the previous generations would be lacking in confidence and spirit.

Nevertheless, existing buildings must be renovated where they are still loved and useful and it is now well established as government housing policy through the grants system that the housing problem will be tackled with renovation and improvement as one of its most important aspects.

1 New and Old: The Mixture

The architect will know, within his own approach to his art, his attitude to the mixture of new with old. His client may hold firm views one way or the other and hopefully the two may coincide. In any case, the existing building's own character and surroundings will impinge on any decisions as to the character and form of the proposals for alteration or extension.

It is perhaps true that where a building is extended in a manner similar to the existing structure, the result may not be noticeable and will, after a little time, appear even to have been part of the original. The merger of new into old naturally makes this work less remarkable than something different in structure, colour or scale.

Although one admires the regularity and consistency of 18th-century town architecture, there is little doubt that today the possibilities, choice and ideas current are more varied than ever before. Far from being stereotyped, the structural and spatial opportunities available to architects today are perhaps all too bewildering to the practitioner. Personal conviction and theory will tend to narrow the choice.

I suggest that the spirit of the building to be extended is the true linking agent in suggesting the architecture of the new extension itself, rather than any overt feature. The architectural languages of today are best used with their grammar and syntax correctly deployed. If the new work has its own integrity and is skilfully done it should in turn complement the old. The two should set off a gentle reaction to their mutual advantage.

ENLARGING A HOUSE BY A SEPARATE BUILDING

It may be that the building to be extended is itself in a state of perfect balanced repose; complete in itself. But the owner wants more space, different facilities, a different aspect. If the proposed extension is of sufficient size, it may be possible to set it away from the parent house and link it tenuously by, perhaps, a glazed passage to set the two buildings away from one another. This will leave the existing building basically as it always was externally, whatever is done to it inside.

I was associated with Kit Evans RIBA in carrying out an extension to a cottage at Singleton in Sussex, where this idea was implemented. The owner required four more bedrooms and two bathrooms. The old flint cottage was inadequate in size to incorporate so much extra space. In any case, the cottage was extremely small and it was decided to take out the first floor and turn the whole shell of the cottage into a living room. The large chimney stack became isolated two-thirds of the way down the room, the space behind becoming the library. The exterior of the cottage was basically unaltered so that the old first floor windows threw light down to the tiled ground floor. The old roof trusses were left exposed and the ceiling boarded. This feeling of height was carried through into the single storey extension, which had boarded ceilings taken up under the pitched roof joists. The two buildings became therefore a pair of approximately the same height, linked by an entrance hall glazed on both sides. Although the glazing for the extension was quite different from the old cottage, we considered its straightforwardness to be apposite for this situation and perhaps even a contemporary equivalent to the old cottage's match-boarded ledged doors and side hung casements (see page 8).

ALTERATIONS WITHIN THE HOUSE SHELL Le Corbusier's use of interlocking sections, double heights, mezzanines, usable roof terraces and general spatial manipulation has had its great effect on ideas not only for new buildings but for alterations to the interiors of houses. The cut away first floor over part of the floor area to give a double height and balcony has become a common way of introducing an exciting spatial experience. Perhaps this cannot all be due to Le Corbusier's work, being also of course a characteristic of many medieval buildings. But some old cottages have very low ceilings less worrying to their early inhabitants because of their shorter stature. Now with our increased size, these spaces can indeed be claustrophobic, though teaching us a lot about the scale of small spaces and dimensions. The cosy English cottage is not to be despised; it is just that standing in a half crouch is tiring after a while and the removal of part of the ceiling and floor above can bring dividends. The same operation, i.e. removal of the first-floor ceiling and its replacement at a higher level such as under the collars to the roof, or even right up to the ridge itself, can be a comparatively simple operation producing a much larger usable volume. A typical example of this approach is given on page 144.

Many barns and large single-space buildings have been converted into dwellings because of the amalgamation of farmsteads into more centralised concerns, or the elimination of village schools. Here the problem is the reverse of the cottage mini-spaces: the large space waiting to be filled.

The large space will almost certainly have roof trusses and these will have their influence on the possibilities. They can be used to hang decks or floors from, or to support floors on their bottom members. This has been done in the example given on page 95 at Coleshill where floors have been placed like decks across the main space to maintain the feeling of the whole volume, connected by straight stair flights. It has also been possible in this case to add the decks from time to time to accommodate the expanding family and its demands for extra space.

This interest in opening up old properties both vertically and horizontally is due to several factors, apart from the aesthetic. With an element of conjecture, I would say that these days there are seldom servants living-in so that the family may have the house entirely to themselves and need less privacy or private rooms for strangers. And, as mentioned before, early 20th-century architects, led by Le Corbusier, have looked at enclosed space in new ways, opening up the rigid cellular room plans of the past, to give those diagonal views and openings so characteristic of contemporary architecture. Encouraging also to this outlook has been the development of central heating, and the various alternative methods available such as warm air in ducts, hot-water radiators, night-storage heaters, night-storage underfloor electric heating (or on day rate), electric wall and ceiling panels, electric fan heaters, apart from slow-burning stoves, etc.

Instead of huddling round the fire, the family can do its 'own thing' in a wholly warmed house and this has contributed to the opening up of spaces.

The kitchen is now not a room shut away out of sight, banished to the old damp basement, but more often the hub of the home, the control centre.

EXTENDING THE HOUSE UPWARDS Raising the roof, or altering the existing roof space is likely to be the most beneficial way of enlarging a city or town house. The existing walls will probably be adequate to take the new superimposed loads.

Existing roof envelope retained

The roof itself may be high enough to form a large enough envelope for new rooms to be inserted within, and with the help of dormers or rooflights, adequate light let in. The extension of the house staircase upwards in its basic formation may not be possible because of head height problems at the landing. A spiral stair or steeper arrangement of flights may be necessary to get up into the attic space. If this does not take place off the main-stair top landing, the existing rooms on that floor will have to be altered. The ceiling rafters will probably not be adequate to take the new floor, live and dead loads and new floor joists laid alongside, inevitably raising the floor level. These can often bear on the ceiling joist wall plates. The attic space may be encumbered with trusses, posts and struts. These structural elements will therefore need to be replaced with another support system if it is necessary to clear the space to form rooms. If there are posts and struts, the purlins will not be adequate on themselves, but perhaps supports could be taken off adequate load-bearing partitions below. The water tank may also have to be repositioned. Although usually attics are altered to provide more space, or a separate flat, they can of course be opened up to the floor below to give double-height spaces over part of whole. The effect of arriving in a space such as this having come up a conventional stair through the usual sequence of spaces can be thrilling, especially if the daylighting or artificial lighting has been cunningly organised. See example 14 in page 149.

Any attic converted to habitable rooms must comply with the by-laws governing top-floor room heights and the regulations concerning means of escape in case of fire may also affect the design (see Chapter 7).

Changing the roof to form a new storey

More often, to provide another floor means the removal of the old roof and the construction of a new one at higher level, whether flat, pitched or of whatever form chosen. The staircase problem will be the same as that noted above. However it is likely that the side or party walls will need to be raised to accommodate the mandatory minimum floor-to-ceiling height of 2.3 m over half the floor area taken at a height of 1 m in London, 1.5 m elsewhere. This will also involve raising chimney stacks where still in use, both those of the house and any adjoining owners' property for which a party wall award will be required. At the front of the property, the parapet or eaves line may have to be maintained to satisfy the town planners, or for aesthetic reasons, and a new top floor is often set back from the façade to maintain this line and to comply with light angles. To make something of this, the new storey can be set back from the parapet to provide a terrace, which is often a delight at the top of a house.

There will be problems with draining rain water from a terrace as often, in London central valley gutter terrace houses, the rain water is taken down the back of the house. Usually the floor joists bear on the front and back walls with the central cross partition taking the centre house loads. This enables a rainwater pipe to be taken from a front terrace gulley in a reasonable fall between the joists to the RWP hopper at the rear. It is advisable to provide cleaning eye access to the pipe as it will probably be buried above a ceiling and below a finished floor. Should the gulley get blocked, the terrace water level could rise dangerously to flood the room. It might be worth-while to provide a water escape route, an overflow pipe, through the parapet at the front to prevent this, placed, say, 4 in (100 mm) above the terrace level. Usually the rear wall can be built up vertically off the existing, unless this is considered to keep too much light off the rear garden, when the new storey could have a pitched roof at that point down onto the existing rear wall.

It is sometimes possible to build the new roof above the existing one before removing the latter. This will reduce to a minimum the period when the rest of the house is open to the elements. The new roof can be built, waterproofed and basically completed before the old is dismantled below it. By building in this sequence, the cost of a temporary roof and tarpaulins may be saved, wholly or partly, the existing house better protected from the weather and more usable during the building operation to the inhabitants as the builders will have their own access to the roof via the scaffolding and their entry into the house can be delayed until a later point in the contract than if the roof is removed before a new one is constructed.

In raising the roof, the cold water tank can be raised to a higher level, possibly in an enclosure on the top of the new roof. Access will be necessary, either by ladder from any terrace at the new floor level, or through a roof light-cum-hatch to the new roof. The cold water tank can be left in its position if that does not inconvenience the new floor plan and there are no sanitary fitments wanted at the new level. Usually, however, a new bath or shower room is wanted to serve the new accommodation, in which case it is probably necessary to raise the tank to the new roof to get enough pressure. In any case, it is not easy to get enough head of water for a shower as if the tank is on the flat roof at a minimum height and the shower head is, say, 6 ft (1800 mm) off the floor, the water head will be only about 2 ft 6 in (762 mm). Showers with electric pumps integrated in them can step up the pressure. Some showers, such as the Mira range, are made non-thermostatic, which enables their simpler mechanism to let the water through with less friction. But if possible, the tank should be built at a height as high as feasible structurally and aesthetically and then the water pressure problem can be reduced. If there are few fitments needing proper pressure and the aesthetic disadvantages of a tank housing on the roof are of importance, the tank can be housed at high level in a cupboard or over the staircase. Or it can be built in a low housing half through the roof, i.e. giving reasonable headroom below with stop cocks etc. within the house, but with the top and ball valve accessible from the roof. This can give a low roof profile if this requirement is important in the circumstances.

By adding a floor to the top of a house it should be remembered that extra loads will be imposed on the existing walls, central or other load-bearing partitions, and thus indirectly on the foundations. Our forefathers were remarkably casual about foundations and usually provided inadequate brick footings. However the extra load is usually well within the capability of the existing walls, and although the District Surveyor or Building Inspector may insist on holes being dug to expose the foundations to assess their size and the bearing ground, it is only on specially difficult ground that underpinning may be necessary to improve the foundations to a standard suitable for the new top storey. There may be evidence that settlement has taken, or is taking place, and therefore special care will be needed in adding an extra storey.

EXTENSION AT THE REAR OR GARDEN SIDE

There may well be an existing extension already on the garden side. Most houses have extended themselves by wash houses, boiler rooms, garden sheds, conservatories and various excrescences often of rather a gimcrack nature.

Peninsular extension

If the house is extended with a 'peninsula' of new construction, which is perhaps the most usual for terrace houses, it will allow light to the existing rear rooms to be left unobstructed if the 'peninsula' is built out from the staircase part of the plan. A two-storey peninsula extension is often the case as the first floor can be reached off the stair half-landing in many cases.

When an extension is made in the above manner, there may be difficulties in maintaining light to the existing staircase which would have been lit from windows on the landings. However, the levels may be such that a fanlight window can be introduced above the new roof level to provide light and the required staircase ventilation.

Often an extension of this type will be built on the boundary and will involve a party wall award and problems of rights of light and overlooking with adjoining owners will arise. (See Chapters 5 and 6.) The dividing garden wall is unlikely to be strong enough, with inadequate foundations, to support a new extension, even single storey, and will need to be taken down and rebuilt, with foundations at a greater depth. This will involve disturbance to the adjoining owner's garden or lean-to sheds or greenhouse built against the old garden wall.

The rooms to be provided in an extension vary very much with the layout of the house. If large enough, a kitchen in this position can allow the cook good supervision of children in the garden and is convenient for serving food outside in a sheltered spot. Alternatively, the boiler room, laundry, workshop and utility spaces are often found there.

A peninsula extension can itself be a connecting link to a larger room or rooms built across the width of the site. If levels allow, this extension could be sunk in the ground to leave its roof level with the garden walls and thus less obtrusive to neighbours. In doing this a small courtyard can be formed between the extension and the main building. With this kind of development, regulations concerning space at the rear of the buildings will apply and be more relevant than usual.

Peninsula development can be more than two storeys, but if built off the staircase landings will mean that light will have to be introduced into the staircase by some method other than fanlights. This can be done by extending the landings of the stair into the new extension and incorporating a side light onto the landing before reaching any room partitions.

Full-width extension

Instead of, or in addition to, a peninsula extension, the house can be extended across its full width. The projection will probably depend on how much light can still be introduced into the centre of the house. There will need to be a large amount of glass to allow adequate light to penetrate into the interior. However, if there is a change of level possible, the extension roof may be dropped a sufficient amount to allow high-level fanlights to be introduced between the existing rooms and the extension. Alternatively, substantial rooflights in the new roof where it abuts the existing house, or a continuous patent glazed light, will help introduce light nearer the centre of the building.

Extensions to the side

Where there is room beside the house to extend it, there is the opportunity to incorporate a garage or to replace an old one with new car space incorporated in a new wing. It may be of course that a garage is not required. The accommodation possible in a side extension is not capable of general discussion here as there are too many unknown factors and too much variety of house plan involved. However, as a side extension would usually be capable of incorporating a separate entrance, it could be designed either initially or later to be a self-contained flat, even a 'granny' flat. This need for the provision of self-contained, safe but compact dwellings for the aged, giving them their own place although supervised by the occupiers of the main house, is usually provided by a side extension because of the independence suggested by a separate entrance.

A side extension may have more than one storey, depending of course on circumstances. If there is a separate flat on the ground floor, the other floor or floors can provide additional accommodation for the main house.

Town planning requirements may well allow a 'granny' flat for a relation of the owners, but not for a separate dwelling unit that might be let or sold on the open market. Planning approval might be conditional on this point. It may be that an obvious independent entrance door might have to be omitted to make the flat integral with the house.

6

2 Design Decisions

The discussions with the client at the initiation of the job are extremely important. The success of the venture will depend to a great extent on these early discussions, as, of course, they do for any building operation whether for a new building or work to an existing one. There will probably be misconceptions on both sides about the expectations of the client and the services the architect or surveyor can provide. Regretfully, the availability of finance is the most important factor for a happy contract.

If you are not careful, a long discussion can ensue about the client's own ideas for the work and all the possible alternatives and optimistic permutations involved, only to find that when finance is mentioned the figure the client has in mind is quite inadequate and would perhaps barely cover the repair and redecoration of the house let alone any extensions or alterations. It is true of course that one can inspire a client to raise further finance for a particularly ingenious and beneficial idea, but it is best that the broad implications of the available funds be discussed at the earliest meeting. The client must take into consideration also the professional fees for architect or surveyor, solicitors, and consultants as well as Value Added Tax on the work, removals, temporary accommodation, carpets, curtains, cookers, dishwashers, washing machines and driers, and special furniture, apart of course from the cost of the finance itself.

The client may produce his own sketches of what he has in mind. These, curiously, seldom show the thickness of a wall but indicate it with a thin line: food for thought for psychologists interested in people and buildings.

However, the client's brief must be built up by mutual preliminary discussion. A visit to his present home, whether it is the one under consideration or not, is beneficial and can tell the designer a lot as to his client's aesthetic interests, or lack of them. It will also show the special arrangements and traditions hallowed within every family and their relevance to the design of their new home. Discussions with the client, husband and wife (or 'husband' and 'wife') will soon reveal who is the driving force behind their desire to convert or alter, who will be putting on any pressure should the way become stony, the going rough, who is in control of the finances or who has access to any trust that will be paying the bills. 'Arbitration' (in the informal sense of the term) will also be necessary to decide the priorities of one side or the other; a delicate matter especially as it will probably be decided by the funds available.

Care should be taken in dealing with the female in the household. Psychologically, I think that having an outside male (or female) querying, prying

Floor plan. House at Singleton, Sussex. Architect Kit Evans and Peter Collymore. The old cottage, at the bottom of the plan was turned into a living room and library, with the old chimney stack forming an island. A kitchen was built into the lower, left hand end. The four new bedrooms with two bathrooms were provided in a separate building joined to the old cottage with a fully glazed link. A double garage was also provided.

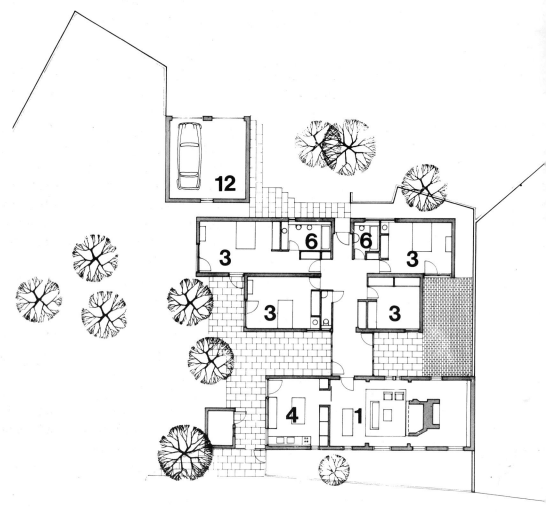

A cross section showing the new building on the left, glazed link in the centre and old cottage on the right. The extension was given high boarded ceilings under the sloping roof joists, with a roof light lighting the circulation space as shown on the section.

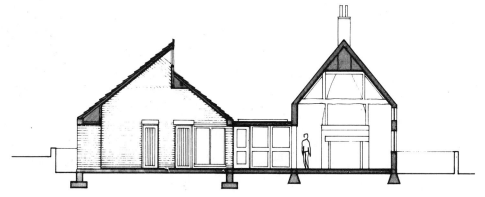

8

into and often disputing her domestic arrangements and proudly-put-forward proposals can bring forth an emotional reaction of some strength immediately or delayed.

The client should be encouraged to write down his own requirements. This, apart from clarifying his verbal instructions, can form a valuable check list and a record of the initial instructions to the architect or surveyor. It will probably save a certain amount of discussion between the latter and each half of the client which can be unproductive. The suggestion I put to one client that he should write an essay on his ideas for the work was rather indignantly declined but there is some value in the idea. However, whatever the client suggests are his needs should be investigated dispassionately. It is often at this point that the basic decisions are taken and here also that the maximum value of an outsider's (the architect's or surveyor's) assessment and re-investigation can be most helpful and influential. Such things as drainage and structural considerations are not likely to be fully understood by the client and his own ideas may not take these into consideration. I have found that a drastic approach to structural changes is not often considered by the owner and drainage not considered at all.

An important matter that should be discussed or assessed early is that of the standard of finish expected by the client with its effect on the finances for the project.

A site visit should be made with the owner to look at the condition of doors, skirtings, architraves, plaster, existing sanitary goods, ironmongery, window frames and glazing bars, etc:

Plaster walls	Will old, possibly uneven, lath-and-plaster walls be acceptable? Warn that when paper is stripped, plaster may come off too. 'Live' plaster ceilings might be saved but better probably to take down and replaster
Doors	Is client willing to pay for burning-off or is paint to be applied over old?
Skirtings, architraves	Will client accept mouldings filled with paint over the years and therefore obliterated? Or is paint to be burnt off and mouldings cleaned out; or is it cheaper to replace old architraves with new?
Windows	Old decayed and damaged glazing bars. Will client want to pay for new or put up with less-than-perfect existing ones? Similarly with moulded frames, panels and architraves
Ironmongery	Are old, inefficient locks, knobs, etc. to be put up with, or are new insisted on?
Flooring	Are existing floors to be repaired or covered up by future flooring? How far are floors to be made good?

This stone barn on the Lancashire hills, was converted by Goad Burton Partnership, Architects, using plain sheets of glass and forthright fenestration in the same spirit as the robust architecture itself.

Naturally, the client should be informed as to the physical state of the building he intends to convert or alter (see Chapter 9 The Preliminary Survey of the Building).

Following the inspection of the premises the architect will have a firm idea of the standard of finish required and what the client is willing to pay for. But he will also have to advise whether the standards are likely to be attained (or whether they are even too low). The costs of various operations and their comparison with alternatives can probably be assessed using a mixture of common sense and experience. For instance, operations where scaffolding is needed obviously cost more than the same operation carried out at ground level, if the scaffolding is needed only for one operation.

If the builder is present there is no reason why his opinion on alternative costs should not be sought. A local builder with knowledge of the construction of vernacular or regional architecture is often of the greatest help in these early stages. He can also discuss the availability of local building materials, matching bricks, tiles, stone, etc.

EXPLORATORY WORK If the alterations are to be carried out to a building into which the owner will move from another, it will probably be occupied by the vendors until shortly before possession by the contractor. In this case it is not easy to make a thorough investigation under carpets, behind fixtures and furniture, and to make trial holes in walls or floors to examine the structural condition hidden from view by the finishes. However, if the building is empty, it would be a very useful exercise to get the builder (who could be one of the tenderers or one to negotiate with) to do some preparatory examination of the fabric. This operation would enable the architect to write a more accurate specification and thus help to cut down the unforeseen problems that can occur and upset at least the financial situation, let alone the planning of the operation.

It would be worth setting aside a sum of money for this exploration work. Suggested parts of a building where works of preliminary investigation might be carried out are as follows:

Hatch to attic	If roof space is closed off with no existing hatch, cut through ceiling in position where hatch could be fitted to gain access for investigation of roof structure and its condition
Plaster	Where plaster to partitions is lined and/or papered, an area should be stripped off to reveal whether plaster behind is 'live', i.e. loosely pinned to backing or structure. Often lining paper when stripped will bring plaster away with it. This will probably mean replastering and can come as an unpleasant surprise unless allowed for in the specification
Floors	Lift a floorboard or two to check joists in cases of deflection, unevenness, points of likely rot (under windows, in corners near party walls, gutters, etc.). In basements or ground floors, check sub floor construction for evidence of rot, adequate ventilation, type of sub floor, sleeper walls, etc.
Fireplaces	Remove any temporary panels to openings to examine fire bricks to enable decision to be made as to retention, revisions, rebuilding, or blocking up
Electrical installation	If the installation is obviously old and inadequate, little need be done in the way of exploration. If there are reasons to keep the layout, perhaps add to it, it can be tested with a Megger. Check the condition of the wiring and equipment by disconnecting typical socket. Hack off plaster patch to check wire conduits or lack of same.
Drainage	Lift manhole covers and check for blockage and general condition. Tests could be done at this exploratory stage (see Defects and Action, Chapter 9). If necessary, excavate in one or two places to check drain runs and their subsoil condition

Walls	If construction is in doubt (i.e. stone-faced, brick-lined, with rubble infill?), cut holes to determine thickness and general construction. If a new opening is required in the proposed alterations, cut trial hole in that position
Pipes	If old or suspect, cut section to check on condition and furring
Generally	Cut away or take apart to examine various areas or parts where defects are suspected

These preliminary physical activities could also be done as a prelude to a general visit by the District Surveyor or Building Inspector. It is worthwhile to get his opinion on any problematical aspects of the proposed work at an early stage. It is best to keep him informed so that he can advise what regulations may be relevant. One should avoid being taken by surprise by unforeseen requirements of the local authorities generally.

A Wiltshire stone house has been extensively altered inside, with a double-height living room acknowledged on the exterior with a new tall window. The end extension, in line with the main house, provides a covered space and storage. Architect: Theo Crosby.

3 Town and Country Planning Acts, and Their Impact on Converting and Extending Houses

Although there were various acts which impinged on town planning (such as the 1909 Act which dealt with factories being built in residential areas and vice-versa), the Act which has formed the basis for, and given rise to, numerous amendments and variations since, was the 1947 Town and Country Planning Act. Later this Act was repealed and replaced with the 1962 Town and Country Planning Act. This in turn gave way to the 1968 Act (following a White Paper of 1967) which amended the 1962 Act in many respects. This became again too complicated and gave rise to the consolidating Town and Country Planning Act 1971. It consolidated the 1962 and 1968 Acts, and a number of other acts as they affect planning (London Government Act 1963, the Control of Office and Industrial Development Act 1965, the Industrial Development Act 1966, the Civic Amenities Act 1967 and others).

Then in 1972 the '71 Act was amended to become the 'Town and Country Planning (Amendment) Act 1972'. This amended among other items the public participation in planning procedures.

LOCAL PLANNING AUTHORITIES: THE CHANGES OF THE LOCAL GOVERNMENT ACT 1972

This Act came into force on 1st April 1974 and allocated the responsibility for planning control to both county and district councils.

Some applications, orders or notices in planning may relate to 'county matters'. A county matter means:

1 The winning and working of minerals or buildings erected in connection with that activity
2 Searches and tests for minerals
3 Use of land for disposing of mineral waste
4 Any development which would conflict with the structure plan, development plan if still in use, be inconsistent with the local plan, or inconsistent with any policy statement of the county council
5 Development affecting a National Park
6 Development or class of development prescribed by the Secretary of State by regulation as being a county matter

Applications for planning permission in respect of general planning control, determinations under Section 53 whether such a permission is required, an established use certificate under Section 94, are to be decided by the district planning authority.

If county planning authorities are determining an application for planning permission, they should afford the district planning authority an opportunity to make recommendations.

District planning authorities are responsible for:

1 The revocation or modification of planning permission, the issuing of an order requiring discontinuation of use, the imposing of conditions on continuance of use, the requiring of alterations or removals of buildings
2 The serving of enforcement or stop notices
3 Keeping a register of planning applications and decisions
4 Dealing with listed buildings, preservation notices, and control of advertisements

IMPLICATION OF PLANNING LAWS ON CONVERSION WORK

In general 'development' requires town planning approval. There are many borderline situations concerning what constitutes 'development', but in conversion work this can be narrowed down to works involving construction which alters the exterior or adds to the existing buildings vertically or horizontally, or changes the use of the building. However, if permission was required for every alteration to a building, there would be a vast bureaucracy necessary to run such an Act. Therefore the General Development Order 1963 was passed, which grants approval automatically to various classes of small works, all as described in Class 1 below. Many minor alterations and extensions to houses are permitted by the Act and therefore do not require formal Town Planning approval.

Approval for change of use is also allowed automatically under the General Development Order for some instances, but formal approval will be necessary if you convert a single family dwelling into flats. Even if the owner lives on the, say, ground, first and second floors and converts and sublets or sells the basement, he will require formal approval for 'change of use' of the building. Similarly if the building is already converted into flats, it will require formal approval for 'change of use' to turn it back into a single family dwelling. And of course, if the building is to be converted into a dwelling and was last used as an office, shop, or for another activity, it will need formal approval for the change.

Generally

Whatever the work proposed, it is well worth while discussing the matter as soon as possible in drawing form, with the local planning authority. As it takes sometimes up to 5 months to get a decision in some London boroughs, it is important to find out at the earliest whether the proposed work requires approval so that an application can be made. A client can be rightfully aggrieved if you should reach a stage where work is in hand, only to find that it has to be delayed for a town planning application to be determined, especially if it then takes 5 months.

A further advantage of early discussion with the planning authority is that divergence of opinion between architect (or surveyor) and planning officer may be capable of resolution or compromise.

As can be seen from the preamble to this section, the planning laws have been revoked, amended, consolidated and revised at frequent intervals to meet changed circumstances and to cure faults in earlier Acts brought to light by their use. Discussion with the planning officer can take account of changes either in the law which may have escaped the architect's or surveyor's notice, and, equally important, to check on the interpretation thereof by the local officers. For instance, it has been found that, in two adjacent London boroughs, opinion has varied completely on the desirability of forming flats in houses. One borough was against forming several units in what was a single family dwelling. The other would not allow a multi-occupation house to be turned back into a single family unit ('change of use'). The two houses were otherwise similar.

Aesthetic control is still a bone of contention. 'Keeping in keeping' is still the practice and, one feels, secret desire of many planning authorities, often carried to absurd lengths when the architecture to be kept 'in keeping' with is not worthy of such a retrograde step. It is a conservatism which has received all too much support from the preservationist lobbies.

ASPECTS OF PLANNING CONTROL LIKELY TO IMPINGE ON THE DESIGN

The following aspects are likely to be considered in relation to an application, by the planning authority:

1 Density, and over-development of the site; the zoning on the local development plan will give the number of persons per acre (or hectare) considered reasonable for the district. The proposed scheme may be considered out of line with this requirement based on the area of the site and the number of persons to be accommodated

2 Aesthetic control. The appearance of alterations or extensions is subject to control both in the design and materials used. Matching materials are often suggested or required, and sometimes samples are required to be deposited at the planning office for approval

3 Change of use. As noted before, the local authority may have a policy which may be for or against the division of houses into flats, which operation requires approval. Similarly, the local authority may have other policies concerning the change of use of the building, which should be investigated

THE GENERAL DEVELOPMENT ORDER 1963

(Reissued as Consolidated Order 1973.) In this order the following are defined as not requiring planning development approval, the permission being implicit in the order itself. The order includes 23 classes of permitted development of which not all are relevant here.

Class I

Permits the enlargement, improvement or other alteration of a dwelling house so long as its cubic content (as ascertained by external measurement) is not increased by more than 1750 ft³ (50 m³) or one tenth whichever is the greater, subject to a maximum of 4000 ft³ (115 m³). This is subject also to the following provisions:

a the height of the building must not exceed the height of the original dwelling house

b no part of the building may project beyond the forward-most part of the original dwelling house

This class also allows the erection within the curtilage of a dwelling house of any building or enclosure (other than a dwelling, garage, stable, loose box or coach house) required for a purpose incidental to the enjoyment of the dwelling house as such.

This class is also subject to a further condition, that the height must not exceed in the case of a building with a ridge roof 12 ft (3.658 m), or in any other case 10 ft (3.048 m)

Class II	Minor building operations such as gates, fences, walls and other means of enclosure, provided that they do not exceed 4 ft (1.219 m) in height when abutting a road used by vehicles or 7 ft (2.134 m) in height in any other case. Under this class the external painting of a building is also authorised provided that it is not in the nature of advertisement
Class III	Authorises a 'change of use' of a building from a general industrial building to a light industrial building. It also permits the change of use of a restaurant to any type of shop (except a fried fish shop, a tripe shop, a pet shop including a bird shop, a cats' meat shop or a shop for the sale of motor vehicles) and also a change of use to any type of shop from the five categories of shop mentioned above, into a shop
Class IV	Gives permission for the erection or construction on land of buildings, plant or machinery needed temporarily in connection with the carrying out of an authorised development. It also gives permission for the temporary use of land for any purpose on not more than 28 days in any calendar year, and permits the erection and placing of moveable structures on the land for the purposes of that use. This permission is applicable to fairs, markets and camping
Class V	Not relevant. This class refers to land not within the curtilage of a dwelling
Class VI	Authorises the carrying out on agricultural land of more than one acre and comprised in an agricultural unit of all the building and engineering operations likely to be undertaken on a normal farm. The provision and alteration of dwellings, however, are not included. Some conditions are attached regarding the size and height of the buildings particularly in the vicinity of aerodromes
Class VII	Forestry buildings and works. Similar permission is given in respect of building and other operations required for forestry

Class VIII	Refers to industrial development
Class IX	Repairs to unadopted streets and private ways
Class X	Repairs to services, such as sewers, underground telephones, etc
Class XI	War-damaged buildings, works and plants. Although the replacement of war-damaged buildings is authorised under this class of permitted development, the Secretary of State, who is entitled to exclude or limit some classes, excluded this class in many areas wishing to keep under control the rebuilding of towns after the war destruction. A similar power of exclusion is given to local authorities with the approval of the Secretary of State

It can be seen that in some 'development' whether of construction or change of use it can be difficult to determine whether town planning approval is necessary or required. Section 53 provides that if any person who proposes to carry out any operation on land or to make any change of use in the land, wishes to have it determined beforehand whether permission is required, he may apply to the local planning authority asking for determination of the question. There is a right of appeal to the Secretary of State against the determination of the local authority and a further right of appeal to the High Court (on limited grounds).

The approval of works under the General Development Order of 1963 (Consolidated Order of 1973) discussed above implies that no formal application for approval to the local planning authority is necessary for the development noted above. This is so in most circumstances, but can be over-ruled if the building or site is in a conservation area.

THE CIVIC AMENITIES ACT 1967 Created the new concept of 'conservation areas'. Before the Act, the only buildings subject to preservation were those listed as being of special architectural or historic interest. These are therefore individual, or small groups of buildings, and are classified according to their assessed architectural value (see later concerning this Act). The idea of the Civic Amenities Act is to extend the idea of preservation to whole areas, districts, or villages, where it is considered that the architectural value of the whole is something special and should have an element of planning control. The Town and Country Planning Act 1971 covered this in Section 277. 'It is a duty of every local planning authority to determine which part of their area are areas of special architectural or historic interest, the character or appearance of which it is desirable to preserve or enhance, and shall designate such areas as conservation areas'. The Secretary of State for the Environment may also direct a local authority to do this. There are now some 1500 conservation areas. Altering or converting houses in conservation areas has its own problems, the local authority being on the whole against drastic changes to the outsides of the buildings unless such alterations are to return the building to its original form and reproduce its original detail. Implicit in the title 'conservation areas' is the theory that a whole area of town or village is worthy of conservation, and therefore that comparatively insignificant buildings (not formally listed as being of special architectural and historic interest) are controlled as to development and alteration by being in a conservation area.

Any application for development, which, in the opinion of the local planning authority, would affect the character or appearance of a conservation area must be published by a notice in a local newspaper and displayed on the site. Members of the public can raise objection to the application. The Town and Country (Amendment) Act 1972 gives the local planning authority power of control over demolition of any building in a conservation area, even if it is not listed. Detailed provisions in respect of the control over buildings in conservation areas are contained in the Town and Country Planning (Listed buildings and buildings in Conservation Areas) Regulations 1972.

Alterations, extensions or even change of use which would normally be considered permitted development under the General Development Order would require Town Planning approval if proposed for a building in a conservation area or if the building is listed as being of special architectural and historic interest.

BUILDINGS OF SPECIAL ARCHITECTURAL OR HISTORIC INTEREST

These are 'listed' by the Secretary of State for the Environment, taking into account not only the architectural quality, but contributions to the historic or architectural interest of any group of buildings, and the desirability of preserving any feature of the building in question. A copy of the list is supplied to the local authority, and is also noted in the Land Charges Register. The legal consequence of listing is that any damage caused to a listed building is an offence.

Even if a building is not formally listed, the local authority may issue a 'building preservation notice' which is valid for 6 months and which lists the building temporarily. The Secretary of State may formally list the building within that time, otherwise the notice lapses.

It is an offence to demolish, alter or extend a listed building without obtaining 'listed building consent'. This is different from town planning approval, which may not be necessary for the alterations proposed. However, if town planning approval is necessary because of the scope of the alterations, 'listed building consent' will also be necessary.

THE APPLICATION FOR PLANNING PERMISSION

Outline planning permission

The developer may like to test his preliminary ideas for carrying out work before committing himself to professional fees for submitting a full detailed application. An application for outline permission can be made usually very simply with a site plan and description of proposals, on the same forms and certificates as for full planning permission. The planning authority will give its approval (or otherwise) on an outline application usually with 'reserved matters' in respect of siting, design and external appearance. The authority is then committed to granting planning permission in some form or other at a later date if it has approved an outline application previously.

Full planning permission

The application is made on the appropriate form, obtained from the local planning authority, together with drawings as required to show and elucidate the scheme. Drawings can be coloured to give an impression of the finished building.

Town planning form

Certificates. The applicant need not have a legal interest in the land in question. He may be a prospective purchaser or lessee but he must submit with his application one of four certificates, which are often part of the form itself.

Certificate A states that the applicant is the estate owner or the lessee of the land in question

Certificate B states that the applicant has given notice to all persons, within the preceding 21 days who had been owners of the land and gives their addresses and names

Certificate C is submitted if some of the persons entitled to the notice cannot be found

Certificate D states that none of the owners can be found

With certificates C and D a notice must be published in a local newspaper.

In addition, a further certificate, usually part of Certificate A, is required stating either that none of the land forms part of an agricultural holding or that a notice has been given to all tenants of agricultural holdings. A false notice can incur a fine of up to £100.

The decision on the planning application (determination of the application)

The local planning authority must send a receipt for the application and should give the decision within two months, or three months if the application affects a trunk road. Only by written consent of the applicant may these periods be extended. You can appeal against an extension of time being requested to the Secretary of State, but there is little point where this applies to conversion work as the appeal procedure is a lengthy one in itself (see later).

The decision can be:

1 Permission granted unconditionally
2 Permission granted subject to conditions
3 Permission refused

If the applicant wishes to appeal to the Secretary of State when permission is refused, he must do so within 6 months. On appeal the Secretary of State may allow or dismiss the appeal, or he may reverse or vary any part of the planning authority's decision, even if not a subject of the appeal.

An appeal is made formally, with arguments put forward on both sides in written form and exchanged. The inspector appointed will afford each party an opportunity to be heard by him, sometimes at a meeting at the site. The inspector issues his decision which is final but may be challenged in the High Court within 6 weeks on a point of law. From instigation of the appeal by the applicant to the receipt of the decision by the inspector may take 9 months or so.

The Secretary of State may, at his discretion, order a public inquiry, which is frequently done in important appeals.

Duration of planning permission

Before 1st April 1969, planning approval was for ever, subject to revocation or modification, and conditions attached by the authority that work should start within a given time.

The 1968 Act stipulated that all permitted development must start within the statutory time (to be begun usually within 5 years). In addition, if the completion of the development is unduly delayed, the planning authority may issue a 'completion notice', to be approved by the Secretary of State. Development permitted before the 1968 Act should begin within 5 years of the start of the Act on April 1st 1969.

In the case of outline planning approval, an application for the approval of reserved matters must be made within 3 years. The development itself must start either within 5 years from the granting of the outline planning permission, or within 2 years of the approval of the reserved matters, whichever is the later.

Revocation or modification of planning permission

This may be done at any time, by the planning authority, but only before the permitted operation has been completed or change of use has taken place.

Such revocation or modification requires confirmation by the Secretary of State, unless the persons concerned agree, and it appears to the local authority that no claim for compensation is likely to arise. The local authority has a duty to pay compensation for revocation and modification of permission based on the applicant's expenditure and loss or damage incurred.

Tree preservation

The planning authority in granting planning permission must ensure that a condition for the preservation or planting of trees is made. The authority has a duty to issue a tree preservation order if it is in the interest of amenity to preserve a tree, group of trees or woodland. Trees subject to an order may be felled if dead, dying or dangerous or insofar as they are a nuisance. An application for consent in respect of a tree preservation order follows the usual planning procedure.

If a local authority intends to make a tree preservation order, it must serve a copy of the order upon the owners and occupiers of the land affected. Objections may be made within 28 days. Contravention may be subject to a fine.

4 Grant Aid in Conversion Work

HOUSING ACT 1974 Under the new Housing Act 1974 which came into force on 2nd December 1974, the whole structure of grant aid for the renovation of houses has been revised. A joint circular from the Department of the Environment (circular 160/74) and the Welsh Office (circular 266/74) elucidates the Act itself. No doubt there will be local authority leaflets to further simplify the contents of Act and circular for general public consumption.

The following is a resume and paraphrase of the circular.

The main provisions of the Act are designed to reinforce two basic aims of the Government's housing policy, aims related to the integrated approach to housing renewal. The two basic aims of the Act are:

1 The need for priority programmes

Local authorities are to concentrate resources more positively than hitherto within housing areas most in need of improvement and upon dwellings which are manifestly sub-standard. Too high a proportion of public spending on improvement has been on dwellings already satisfactory (i.e. at or above the former '12-point' standard) and to replacing or adding to existing amenities in cases where this was desirable but by no means essential. The Act encourages selection of urgent priorities by providing extra powers and preferential rates of house renovation grants in housing action areas and general improvement areas. Circulars on Housing Action Areas, Priority Neighbourhoods and General Improvement Areas are in preparation at this time of writing, by the Department of the Environment. As part of the drive towards greater selectivity, the Act restructures the grant system to prevent abuses and to direct available help towards the rehabilitation of dwellings still lacking basic amenities or in serious disrepair.

2 The need to see renewal as a continuous process

The aim is to transform the run-down residential areas of our towns and cities into decent civilized neighbourhoods by a careful mixture and phasing of redevelopment and rehabilitation which would result in gradual and continuous urban renewal over the years.

Grants may henceforth be given over a very wide range of house condition. Although the Act specifies requirements as to standards of work and the estimated life of the dwelling after renovation, authorities are empowered to waive or reduce these requirements in individual cases. For example, a grant might be made towards a bath or W.C. in a dwelling due to be demolished in the not-too-distant future thus making life tolerable meanwhile for the family concerned. This would help to stop designated clearance areas being blighted when development schemes and rehousing arrangements are postponed.

Part VII of the Act covers the four types of house renovation grant now in force.

1 IMPROVEMENT GRANTS

Available at the discretion of the local authority for works normally of a high all-round standard for the improvement or conversion, plus repair, of properties with a good life ahead of them. Authorities may fix grant up to a maximum appropriate percentage of the eligible expense. The Government has announced its intention to raise by Order, the limits of eligible expense in Section 64 of the Act to £3200 in normal cases and to £3700 where a house of three or more storeys is being converted.

2 INTERMEDIATE GRANTS

Generally obtainable by owners as of right for the installation of missing standard amenities and the execution of repairs. The maximum eligible expense for intermediate grants is £700 for the provision of standard amenities and £800 for repairs; grants are fixed by reference to the appropriate percentage of eligible expense.

3 SPECIAL GRANTS

Available at the discretion of the local authority for the installation of standard amenities in houses in multiple occupation at a maximum appropriate percentage of the rates of eligible expense set out in Schedule 6 of the Act.

4 REPAIRS GRANTS

Available at the discretion of the local authority for the repair of dwellings (and not being works associated with the improvement or provision by conversion of dwellings) within Housing Action Areas and General Improvement Areas in cases where the authority thinks it appropriate after taking into account the capacity of the applicant to finance the work without grant aid. This grant may be fixed by the authority up to a maximum appropriate percentage of eligible expense which itself may not exceed £800.

COMPULSORY IMPROVEMENT NOTICES

Part VII of the Act contains the new and strengthened provisions relating to compulsory improvement powers exercisable by local authorities in Housing Action areas and General Improvement Areas, and otherwise.

DWELLINGS PROVIDED AFTER 2nd OCTOBER 1961

Applications for grants for houses constructed after the above date will not be generally 'entertained'.

GRANT APPLICATIONS

The application must contain the following:
1 Plans showing the dwellings or dwellings before and after improvement or conversion
2 A specification of the proposed works
3 In the case of dwellings in respect of which a certificate of availability for letting has been provided by the applicant, a statement of what housing arrangements, if any, are to be made for any existing tenants and their households during and after improvement
4 A statement that the dwelling was built before 2nd October 1961
See later for other requirements of applicants

APPLICATIONS WHICH MAY NOT BE ENTERTAINED

1 An application which includes works for insulating a dwelling against heat loss

2 An application for an improvement grant which relates to a dwelling in respect of which a previous improvement grant has been paid during the period of 30 years immediately preceding the date of application and where the previous grant had been intended to bring the dwelling up to the full required standard

3 An application for an improvement grant for the provision of a dwelling by the conversion of premises which do not, at the date of application, comprise at least one house

In relation to **1** above, applications from elderly or disabled persons would be given sympathetic consideration for grant aid towards roof insulation. In relation to **2** above, in cases where a previous grant had not been intended to bring a dwelling up to the full required standard, a further grant may be given, account being taken of the amount of the earlier grant paid.

The restriction in **3** above is necessary to cover those cases where the rateable value limitation does not apply, e.g. the conversion of barns, oast houses, railway stations, etc. The housing authority may decide that a grant towards improvements in such buildings would be acceptable, having regard to general evidence as to the owner's financial means.

STANDARD OF DWELLINGS

The dwelling must:

1 be substantially free from damp

2 have adequate natural lighting and ventilation in each habitable room

3 have adequate and safe provision throughout for artificial lighting and have sufficient electric socket outlets for the safe and proper functioning of domestic appliances

4 be provided with adequate drainage facilities

5 be in a stable structural condition

6 have satisfactory internal arrangement

7 have satisfactory facilities for preparing and cooking food

8 be provided with adequate facilities for heating

9 have proper provision for the storage of fuel (where necessary) and for the storage of refuse

10 conform with the specifications applicable to the thermal insulation of roof spaces laid down in part F of the Building Regulations in force at the date of the grant approval

The above ten points replace the former '12 point' standard of the previous grant regulations.

Appendix B of circular 160/74

MATTERS COMMON TO ALL GRANTS

On none of the matters dealt with in this Appendix is it the Secretary of State's intention to impose rules to which local authorities must conform: on the various issues discussed in this Appendix authorities have wide discretion to decide whether or not they will approve grant aid, and, in certain cases, to what extent.

Standard amenities: ancillary works

The intermediate grant, like the former standard grant, does not cover ancillary expenditure related to the provision of a standard amenity, e.g.

the bringing in of a water main to a dwelling for the first time or the installation of a septic tank. However, this part of the work can be covered by an improvement grant.

Appropriate percentage of grant

It should be noted that for improvement, repairs or special grants it is open to local authorities to approve grants at percentages lower than the maximum appropriate percentages specified in section 59 (1) should they so wish. Under section 80 of the Act, however, a local authority fixing grant at less than the appropriate percentage is required to state to the applicant its reasons for so doing.

Undue hardship

Where a dwelling is in a housing action area, the local authority can increase the percentage payable on improvement and repairs from the normal limit of 75% to 90% if the applicant would have undue hardship in carrying out the work. Each application to be considered carefully on its merits.

Evidence of financial resources is to be treated in strictest confidence.

Certificates of future occupation

Under Section 60 of the Act, applicants are normally required to submit a certificate of future occupation with their applications for grants other than special grants. The applicant must certify that he intends to reside in the improved dwelling as an owner-occupier or let it. Special provision is made for dwellings occupied or kept available for occupation by a member of the agricultural population in pursuit of a contract for service.

The provisions of this section should in particular prevent grants being approved for second homes or which are being improved by property companies, prior to being sold for owner-occupation.

The owner-occupier must, on his 'certificate of owner-occupation' state that he will live in the house for five years. Provision is made for persons (such as on retirement) to improve a dwelling for subsequent use as their main dwelling during one year, when they may well own two houses during the conversion period.

An applicant who is, or intends to become, the landlord of a dwelling to be improved must provide a 'certificate of availability for letting' which will state that he intends, throughout the period of 5 years beginning with the certified date, that the dwelling will be let, or kept genuinely available for letting as a residence.

Grant conditions

If the use made of the improved dwelling throughout the period of the conditions is not consistent with the intention stated in the certificate, the grant is repayable with compound interest.

Certified date section 75

This new concept requires that the local authority certify the date when the improved dwelling first becomes fit for occupation. This codifies the situation in relation to the five year period and 'grant conditions'.

Repayment of grant on breach of conditions

Repayment of the grant is required if the certificates are flouted. However, there are occasions when dwellings are sold by an owner-occupier because of circumstances (moving job, increasing family). In this case local authorities might not demand any repayment.

Each case ought to be considered on its merits but local authorities may consider it appropriate to demand repayment of an amount which reflects that proportion of the conditions period which remains unexpired.

Revision of grant after approval

An increased, further, estimate for the work required can be considered by the local authority who can redetermine the amount of grant, if it is considered that the applicant could not proceed with the improvements, through no fault of his own, because of increased estimates. Local authorities are advised to exercise this power only if:

1 the original contractor is no longer prepared to carry out the work
2 the failure on the part of the contractor was due to matters beyond the control of the applicant
3 the further estimate submitted is from a different contractor

Grants not payable after property is sold

No grant shall be paid if an applicant relinquishes his interest in the dwelling before the date certified by the local authority as the date on which the dwelling concerned first became fit for occupation after completion of the works.

IMPROVEMENT GRANTS

Disabled persons

If the dwelling is to be occupied by a registered disabled person, an improvement grant can cover works required for his welfare, accommodation or employment where the existing dwelling is inadequate or unsuitable for those purposes.

Rateable value limits

This is a new concept for limitation of premises for grant aid in the case of improvement grants. It does not apply to an application for an intermediate, repair or special grant, nor to a dwelling or dwellings improved for letting. But for owner-occupation, a dwelling must have a rateable value below £300 in London, £175 in the rest of England and Wales.

Enlargements and extensions

The provision of extra living or bedroom space by extension or loft conversion is not considered as a high priority for grant aid. Provision for a first bathroom or adequate kitchen by enlargement would be more frequently considered. The theory is that if the house is too small, the owner should move or pay for the extension of bed or living rooms himself. Exception could be made for dwellings in isolated positions where alternative accommodation is not easy to find.

Fire Escapes

Fire escapes and means of escape from fire may be accepted as part of the eligible cost of the works for improvement grant purposes.

Electrical rewiring

The renewal of existing wiring is regarded as replacement and should not attract improvement grant unless carried out in conjunction with other improvements and accepted by the local authority as necessary to enable the dwelling to achieve the relevant standard. The installation of electric lighting or a power supply for the first time may, however, be properly regarded as an improvement.

Central heating

Grant towards space heating installation costs up to Parker Morris standards may be given when this forms part of the cost of a scheme for converting property into flats or improving a dwelling. However a grant should not be given in the Secretary of State's opinion, for central heating on its own or linked with other inessential improvements.

Parker Morris standards

Although Parker Morris standards are intended as a minimum guide to new building standards, grants will be made in conversion work if that work is to higher standards than those of Parker Morris if the result would be worth the cost.

Water and drainage

House renovation grants are available only for works within the curtilage of a dwelling. However, bringing in mains water for the first time or running drains to an existing sewer or to, and including, a septic tank or cesspool would be likely to get grant aid. The replacement of mains supply or internal piping or a change over from septic tank or cesspool to main drainage ought not, in the Secretary of State's view, attract grant if it does not form part of a comprehensive scheme of improvement.

Repairs and replacements

The proportion of an improvement grant that may relate to repairs and replacements remains limited to a maximum of 50% of the estimated expense. These repairs and replacements must be those needed to attain the relevant standard of improvement to the dwelling.

The local authority may use its power to substitute a higher amount of estimated expense because of unforeseen works that arise after approval.

Higher amounts of improvement grant

The Secretary of State may substitute a higher amount than the relevant limit of the eligible expense if he is satisfied that there are good reasons for doing so with respect to a particular case.

Applications for higher limits to be approved in individual cases may be submitted to the appropriate regional office of the Department of the Environment or the Welsh Office, and will be considered on their merits.

In particular, works of improvement to listed buildings come into this category, although grants for repairs are also available under the Historic Buildings Acts.

INTERMEDIATE GRANTS   This replaces the former 'standard' grant but in addition to assisting with the cost of providing missing basic amenities, the grant may also provide help towards the cost of repairs and replacements.

Disabled persons

Sections of the Act 56 (2) (b) and 65 (3) incorporate special provisions relating to registered disabled persons. For an intermediate grant, the normal requirement that the dwelling should have been without the standard amenity concerned for not less than 12 months need not apply, so long as the existing amenity is inaccessible to that person because of his disability.

Estimates

Intermediate grants unlike the former standard grants, are not paid on actual costs but are based on estimates.

Relevant standard

The conditions to be fulfilled for a dwelling to attain the relevant standard are set out in section 66. Local authorities are placed under a duty to pay grant to an applicant provided various requirements of the Act are satisfied. There is a requirement to prevent the payment of grant where standard amenities have been removed in order to claim grant for new ones.

Repairs and replacements

The introduction of the cost of repairs or replacements into the grant calculation means that the local authority must make the necessary judgement before the work is carried out. They will have to decide on the extent and expense of the works of repair or replacement needed and to notify the applicant of its decision.

Relationship with compulsory improvement notice

A compulsory improvement notice automatically qualifies the owner for the payment of an intermediate grant, even if those works are to a reduced standard.

SPECIAL GRANTS   ### Circumstances in which appropriate

A special grant could be given to provide basic amenities in houses of multiple occupation where there is no immediate prospect of it being divided into separate flats in a thorough-going manner. A case in point would be that of several families sharing one sink and W.C. in a large undivided house. A special grant might be given for additional sinks, W.C.s with water supplies, in order to make life more tolerable, and to relieve bad conditions. They are not intended to encourage undivided multiple occupation.

For special grants a fixed bath or shower must be in a bathroom; no requirement is made about the location of the water closet.

An estimate of the cost will be necessary for a special grant as with an intermediate grant. Special grants do not cover the cost of repairs or replacement arising in respect of houses in multiple occupation.

REPAIR GRANTS   These grants are only available in Housing Action Areas and General

Improvement Areas and are intended to help owners with limited means to carry out basic repairs that they would not otherwise be able to finance. They are entirely discretionary, but could be as much as 90%. It is for local authorities to determine what standard of repairs might be grant aided in these circumstances.

APPROPRIATE PERCENTAGE

The appropriate percentage is the rate at which a grant is made towards the eligible cost of the work. Previously it was set at an overall rate of 50%, with 75% in development areas.

The new rates are:

1 In the case of a Housing Action Area   75%
2 In the case of a General Improvement Area   60%
3 In any other case   50%

The maximum eligible expenditure figures are given elsewhere.

In the case of a house in an Housing Action Area, if the local authority consider that the owner cannot carry out the relevant works without undue hardship, they may treat the appropriate percentage as increased to a maximum of 90% or whatever increase they think fit.

If after an application is made for a grant to a dwelling, which is shortly included in a new Housing Action Area, the application is permitted to be withdrawn and resubmitted, as long as the work has not been begun.

PROCEDURE

Grants are paid when the work is completed, and approved by the inspector. However, the owner can apply for the grant to be paid in instalments. These are usually based on the architect's interim certificates or an inspection of the work done at that time.

An application for a grant will consist of a form to be completed by the applicant or agent, together with the items for which aid is claimed, set out together with the intended builder's prices for each of these items. Some authorities require tenders to be obtained from a minimum of three contractors, others will require only figures from a contractor chosen by the owner (or his agent). As it is not always clear what items are considered worthy of aid, it is best to get the whole specification for all the work priced up in the margin by all the tenderers, or one selected contractor, and this can be submitted as a whole for the authority to select those items worthy of aid. This can be advantageous as the local authority may pick out items that the applicant had not realised were aidable. In addition, the application will need to include drawings to illustrate the proposals, a note of professional fees to be charged on the cost of the work, evidence that town planning approval has been obtained or a letter confirming that town planning approval was not required, evidence that building byelaw approval has been obtained, evidence of ownership (i.e. copy of the title deeds or a solicitor's letter), evidence of any other approvals obtained such as drainage approval, underground room regulations approval etc.

In addition, provisional sums included in the specification must be based on actual quotes obtained. Therefore quotes for electrical work or a central heating installation would need to be available at the time of the application and copies of them submitted.

It will be obvious that by the time an application for a grant can be made, the whole contract will be at the stage where the design and working drawings are done, the tenders received and permissions obtained. In other words, the work could be started on site. However, it is one of the requirements of grant aid that no work whatsoever may be started on site until the grant application has been formally approved. As an application often takes two months to receive approval, it is a frustrating and expensive delay for the owner.

However, once an application has been made, the local authority may relent and allow work to be started if that work is to prevent the building deteriorating. The sort of operation that might be permitted at this stage is the repair of a leaking roof or its renewal, eradication of dry rot, wet rot or insect attack, or other fault likely to cause deterioration of the fabric while the grant application is being considered.

The reasons for not applying for a grant where one is available are worth consideration. As noted above, the delay in obtaining permission to start the work can be frustrating and also expensive. The house will probably have been bought by then and the owner, if he is not already living in it, will be paying for two homes. In these days of inflation, the cost of the building work may go up between the time of applying for and receiving permission to start. The gaining of a grant may involve the owner in more basic building work to comply with the grant requirements than he can afford even with grant aid.

The delay in gaining approval for a start on the work will mean that the builder whose figures have been submitted for approval may himself be busy elsewhere by the time permission is granted. However, as noted above, badly defective parts of the building may be attended to before formal approval is received, as long as this is cleared beforehand with the local authority.

EXCHEQUER GRANTS The Secretary of State for the Environment has the power to make grants for the maintenance and repair of buildings of 'outstanding' architectural or historic interest. As comparatively few buildings qualify for this distinction, the scope of these grants is limited. Listed buildings do not automatically qualify for a Historic Buildings Grant, but it naturally improves their chances if they are.

The Secretary of State is advised on the making of grants by the Historic Buildings Councils for England, Scotland and Wales appointed in 1953. Their function is to keep the Secretary of State informed about the general state of preservation of buildings of outstanding historic or architectural interest and to advise him on the making of grants towards the repair or maintenance of such buildings or their contents, or towards the acquisition of buildings under Section 50 of the Town and Country Planning Act 1968 and Section 71 of the 1962 Act, by local authorities or the National Trust. In 1971 the Government provided funds for this purpose up to £1,000,000. Only buildings of outstanding interest are eligible, but a building with particularly outstanding features might still be considered, even if its general character was not outstanding. Application for one of these grants is made by letter to the Secretary of the Historic Buildings Council for England, Scotland or Wales, and may be made either by a private owner, public body or local authority unable to carry out the work from its own resources. These grants cannot be made retrospectively.

This row of houses at Skipton, Yorkshire, was in great danger of destruction owing to its bad condition. A local campaign to save it encouraged a local builder to convert it into houses, to the design of Wales, Wales and Rawson, Architects. The canal-side architecture appears to have been well worth saving.

5 Party Structures

In London and Bristol, the rights of adjoining owners in relation to works to party structures are governed by local regulations. In most of the rest of the country these matters are considered covered by rights in Common Law.

In London party structures are covered by Part VI of the London Building Acts (Amendment) Act 1939 which deals with the practical issues involved in the erection, maintenance and use of party structures. The legal title to a structure is not affected and all easements and rights are preserved.

In Bristol party walls are governed by Sections 24 to 32 of the 1847 Bristol Improvement Act amended by the Bristol Corporation Act 1926, which provides for party wall awards, thickness of party walls and arches, and joint contributions.

PARTY STRUCTURE Is a party wall, floor, partition or other structure separating buildings or parts of buildings approached only by separate staircases or entrances from outside the building. Tenancy separations in blocks of flats and maisonettes are therefore normally excluded.

PARTY WALL Section 44 gives a special definition of 'party wall':
1 A wall which forms part of a building and stand on lands of different owners
   Projection of any artificially formed support on which the wall rests on to land of any adjoining owner does not make the wall a party wall.
2 Any part of any other wall as separates buildings belonging to different owners

PARTY FENCE WALL This is a wall that is not part of a building but which stands on the lands of different owners and is used or constructed for separating such lands. It does not include a wall constructed on one's own land, of which only artificially formed supports project on to the adjoining land. Thus rights of adjoining owners do not arise where only the foundations project on to the adjoining land if the wall concerned is a boundary wall, not being part of a building, but they do arise if such wall separates buildings belonging to different owners.

PROCEDURE A special procedure has to be followed if the building owner wishes to invoke his rights under the Act. These are more extensive than the limited rights he has at Common Law, and as regards existing structures, may be summarised thus:

31

1 Where a structure is defective, he may repair, make good, thicken or underpin it, or demolish and rebuild it
2 If he wishes to build against it and it is of insufficient height or strength, he may rebuild it subject to making good all damage to adjoining property, and raising the height as necessary of chimneys
3 He may carry out all necessary incidental works to connect with the adjoining premises

Section 46 of the Act elaborates on these rights. Section 50 deals with the underpinning of independent buildings and confers valuable rights on both adjoining owners.

The first step in the process is for the building owner to serve a 'Party Structure Notice' upon adjoining owner or owners, except where their prior written consent has been given or the work is necessary as the result of a dangerous structures notice. The owner may of course do this through his agent (architect, surveyor) and in fact would be well advised to do so as the handling of these forms requires specialist knowledge. The RIBA publish precedent notices (forms A to G). The 'Party Structures Notice' contains particulars of the proposed works and is normally accompanied by a party wall drawing, although a drawing need only be served where it is proposed to use special foundations, i.e. foundations in which steel beams or rods are used to spread the loads. The notice should be served at least two months before the work is to be started in the case of a party structure, or one month in the case of special foundations or a party fence wall. The adjoining owner has the right to serve a counter notice requiring the carrying out of additional works for his protection.

The adjoining owner may, in fact, consent to the proposed works under Section 49. If an owner does not so express his consent in writing to a notice or counter notice within 14 days of service, a 'difference' is deemed to have arisen between the parties. Often, to safeguard the parties a 'difference' has not in fact arisen but for the sake of allowing the normal procedure to follow, with the drawing up of an award and the appointment of surveyors (or architects) to represent each party, it is agreed amicably that there is a 'difference'. The special procedure to be followed for settlement of differences is in effect an arbitration and is contained in Section 55. This enables the parties to agree to the appointment of an agreed surveyor who will make an award upon the difference. This is not usual. In practice each party appoints his own surveyor (who can be an architect) and the difference is settled by negotiation between them and they make a joint award. There is provision for the two nominated surveyors to call in a third who acts as an intermediary, should the original two not reach agreement.

When the party wall award has been agreed it is engrossed (expressed in legal form) and executed in duplicate, each copy being signed and witnessed by the two surveyors (or architects).
The award will deal with the supervision of the works and the cost. Normally costs will be borne by the building owner, but this is not necessarily the case. The award can be challenged by an appeal to the County Court within 14 days of issue, or even by appeal to the High Court.

Expenses in respect of party structures are dealt with by Section 56. Where works are for the benefit of both owners (normally when a party structure is in disrepair) the costs are shared proportionately. The adjoining owner may also be liable to contribute towards the costs when he makes any use of the works as compared with the use when the works were begun. Such a right of contribution does not exist at Common Law. The costs of the party wall itself are not included under expenses, as these are dealt with in the award itself. Expenses to be apportioned include professional fees and district surveyor's fees.

Any works which are carried out by a building owner under the provisions of the Act are subject to four general conditions:

1 The work is not to be carried out in such a way or at such a time as to cause unnecessary inconvenience to the adjoining owner or occupier

2 Where any part of the adjoining land or building is laid open, the building owner must erect and maintain at his own expense proper protective hoardings to the adjoining owner's property

3 The works must comply with the London Building Acts and By-laws

4 The works must be in accordance with any plans, sections and particulars agreed between the owners or approved by their surveyors in the party wall award. Any deviation must be agreed between the two surveyors

THE FORM OF THE AWARD There is no prescribed form of award, but the following layout is suggested for a typical situation:

PARTY WALL AWARD UNDER PART VI OF THE LONDON BUILDING ACTS (AMENDMENT) ACT, 1939.

IN THE MATTER OF the Party Wall between premises known as …………………………… on the North side of the Wall and premises known as ………………………… on the South side therefore, which site is to be developed by the erection of a block of flats, S. O. Else Esq. of ………………………… being and being hereinafter referred to as the Building Owner and the A. N. Other & Co. being one of the Adjoining Owners and hereinafter referred to as the Adjoining Owner …………………………

WHEREAS the Building Owner proposes to carry out certain building operations affecting the said Party Wall and did on the …… day of …………… 19…… serve on the Adjoining Owner a Notice of his intention to make good and repair the Party Wall if defective or out of repair; to cut away the chimney breasts on the Building Owner's side of the Party Wall and make good the Wall thereafter; to underpin, thicken and raise the Party Wall and carry up the existing flues and chimney stacks of the Adjoining Owner on the Wall; to carry out any works necessary to connect the Party Wall to his building; and to do any other works necessary or incidental to all or any of the foregoing, all the particularised works being shown on a Drawing accompanying the said Notice AND WHEREAS no consent having been expressed by the Adjoining Owner within fourteen days of the service of the Notice a difference is deemed to have arisen between the Building Owner and the Adjoining Owner AND WHEREAS in pursuance of section 55 of the Act above recited the Building Owner has appointed …………………

of .... to be his Surveyor and the Adjoining Owner has appointed
.... of .... to be his Surveyor and the above
appointed Surveyors have selected .... of .... as
Third Surveyor

NOW we the undersigned being Two of the above mentioned Three
Surveyors, *without prejudice to any other rights of the parties or to the rights
of any other persons,*

DO HEREBY AGREE AND AWARD as follows:—

(1) That the wall coloured Pink on Drawing A as defined in clause (2)
hereof is wholly a Party Wall standing to a greater extent than the
projection of its footings on the land of both Owners and is in all
respects sufficient for the existing purposes of the Adjoining Owner
but is not sufficient for the purposes of the Building Owner without
underpinning, thickening and raising upon the same.

(2) That the Drawing lettered A annexed hereto and signed by the
Signatories of this Award, hereinafter referred to as Drawing A,
and the Specification lettered B annexed hereto and similarly signed,
hereinafter referred to as Specification B, show and specify the
particularised proposals set out in the Notice of the Building Owner
modified as the Signatories hereto have agreed and awarded that they
may be carried out.

(3) That the works referred to in clauses 4, 6 and 7 of this Award shall
not be carried out except in accordance with Drawing A and Specification B.

(4) That the Building Owner may underpin, thicken, raise upon and
bond into the Party Wall without rebuilding the same, but that the
underpinning and thickening shall be completed as far as may be
before any work of raising or cutting away (otherwise than for underpinning and thickening) is carried out.

(5) That it is agreed that the building owner has a statutory duty to
provide proper shoring, screens and other temporary works as may
be necessary to protect the adjoining owners premises.

(6) That the Building Owner may cut away the chimney breasts on his
side of the Party Wall.

(7) That the Building Owner may, and if the raising of the Party Wall is
carried out, shall raise the chimney stacks and flues of the Adjoining
Owner's premises built into or onto the Party Wall to a height of
three feet above the highest point of the roof of the Building Owner's
proposed building within 20 feet thereof.

(8) That the Party Wall is in a satisfactory state of repair and maintenance
for the purposes of the Adjoining Owner but that the Building Owner
may and shall carry out any repairs thereto necessary for his building
if erected.

(9) That no loads shall be imposed on the Party Wall except as shown on
Drawing A.

(10) That the whole of the works to which this Award relates shall be carried out during ordinary working hours or such other hours as any two of the surveyors may from time to time agree and award and that in the execution of the work all reasonable consideration shall be given to the convenience of the occupiers of the Adjoining Owner's premises.

(11) That the works shall be commenced within two months and so far as may be completed within four months of the date of this Award or such other periods as may be determined by surveyors from time to time.

(12) The Building Owner shall remove all debris, surplus materials, plant and scaffolding from or from the vicinity of the Adjoining Owner's premises as soon as reasonably practicable.

(13) The Building Owner shall give not less than three day's notice to the Adjoining Owner's surveyor of the intended date of commencement or resumption after discontinuance for more than seven days of work to which this Award relates.

(14) That the Building Owner shall make good all damage occasioned by him to the Adjoining Owner's premises.

(15) That the Adjoining Owner's surveyor shall have full and free access to the works during reasonable hours of the daytime during the progress of the works.

(16) That in accordance with the terms of reference we have dealt only with matters arising out of the London Building Act and have not considered any question of easements affecting either property.

(17) That the Building Owner shall pay unto the Adjoining Owner's surveyor the sum of £——— as his fee in connection with the making of this award and the supervision of the works to which it relates on behalf of the Adjoining Owner and shall also pay the cost of stamping this Award and its Counterpart. Upon these payments being made the Adjoining Owner's surveyor shall hand the stamped Counterpart to the Building Owner's surveyor.

(18) That the Building Owner shall pay the reasonable costs of the Adjoining Owner's surveyor in respect of any variations which may be agreed in respect of the works.

(19) That the Building Owner's surveyor shall pay the reasonable additional costs of the Adjoining Owner's surveyor in respect of any unusual delay in the execution of the works, the amount to be determined by the surveyors.

(20) That there is no difference between the Building and Adjoining Owners relative to the before-mentioned Notice at the date of this Award which has not been dealt with herein, but power is reserved to the surveyors to make a further award in respect of any further difference which may arise.

(21) This award shall become null and void if the works to which it relates have not been commenced within the time or substituted time provided for in clause (11).

As witness our hands this .... day of .... 19...
Witness to the Signature of ....
Surveyor to the Building Owner.

Witness..
Description ....
Address..
Witness to the Signature of ....
Surveyor to the Adjoining Owner.

Witness..
Description ....
Address..

A kitchen and dining-room extension in Kent. The raising of the dividing unit off the floor opens up the space and, together with the neat details, gives the room its special quality. Architect: Adrian Gale.

6 Easements, Rights of Light, Ancient Lights, Overlooking

RIGHTS OF LIGHT

There is no right to light generally, but only in respect of some definite opening such as a window or skylight. The owner of a dominant tenement (a plot of land held by an owner, freeholder or leaseholder) has a right only to such amount of light as is necessary for ordinary purposes. If an owner has enjoyed many years use of an exceptional amount of light, it does not prevent an adjoining owner from building so to reduce that light. The decision as to whether or not enough light is left for ordinary purposes must therefore depend on personal observation and even scientific methods for measuring light, as well as the 45° rule for measuring from the centre of a window.

If there is a blocked window or skylight and light could be obtained from from it, this can be taken into consideration as an available light source.

If a dispute arises between adjoining owners, the matter can only be settled in a court of law if the owners cannot reach agreement.

ANCIENT LIGHTS

The Prescription Act 1832 as amended by the Right of Light Act 1959 provided that an absolute right of light could be obtained after 20 years uninterrupted use. Because of the possibility of prescriptive rights being acquired over bomb damaged sites, the 1959 Act provided a temporary extension to 27 years for actions alleging infringement beginning before that date.

To prevent a right of light being established the old method was to erect a temporary screen or hoarding to interrupt the 20 year uninterrupted span. The 1959 Act allows that a theoretical wall can be registered as a local land charge.

7 Fire, and its Bearing on the Design of Conversions and Alterations of Existing Buildings

AUTHORITIES TO BE CONSULTED

In London this matter is dealt with by the Inner London Boroughs themselves, this function being delegated from the G.L.C. Building Regulation Division (Middlesex House, Vauxhall Bridge Road, S.W.1.). Where the alterations concern buildings which contain accommodation other than flats and tenements, e.g. shops with flats above, application must be made to the G.L.C. as noted above.

Outside London application on these matters is made through the building control departments of the local authority. They will discuss the various aspects of fire prevention and escape of a project with the local fire prevention officer at the Fire Brigade, who will make his comments, both mandatory and advised, to the owner or his agent through the building inspector or building control officer.

MEANS OF ESCAPE: REGULATIONS

The Building Regulations describe this matter under Section E, the Building Standards (Scotland) (Consolidation) regulations 1971 under Part E, with parts D and F referring to structural fire precaution and chimneys, flues, etc. respectively.

The London Building Acts (Amendment) Act 1939 under Part V Section 35 describes what is required for the G.L.C. area. The G.L.C. also has a code of practice of its own Means of Escape in Case of Fire at houses in multiple occupation prepared to assist those requiring approval of their proposals for means of escape in case of fire for alterations in forming flats. This G.L.C. code relates to the Housing Act 1961, Section 16.

The theory behind all these regulations is the saving of life rather than the buildings themselves. It is the protection of the escape route, or routes, of a building from the effects of fire and smoke that is the prime consideration. If you are sleeping (for example) on an upper floor of a building, and a fire breaks out on that or another floor, you need to be able to escape within a reasonable time to a safe spot outside the building. The regulations stipulate that this escape route must be able to resist the fire for $\frac{1}{2}$ hour. This involves construction of the enclosing walls of the escape route with fire resisting materials and construction as described in the Building Regulations for that part of Britain.

FIRE RESISTING DOORS

In addition, doors on to the escape route must be fire resisting (again $\frac{1}{2}$ hour) and self-closing. This is so that if a fire breaks out on, say, a lower floor, the escaper can get past it on the escape route without injury within $\frac{1}{2}$ hour of its being subjected to fire on its inner, room, face. New doors can be fitted which are $\frac{1}{2}$ hour fire resisting; existing doors can be brought up to that standard by facing the inner, room, side with fire resistant material as long as the timber of the door and its frame is already of the required thickness. It is sad that pannelled doors have to be faced over in this way. However, if the stiles, rails and frames are not less than $1\frac{3}{4}''$ thick (44.45 mm), the panels can be removed, asbestos or similar sheet applied and the panels replaced to form a $\frac{1}{2}$ hour fire resistant sandwich. These doors must also be self-closing; they must have closers either morticed into the stile or applied on the face so that the door will shut firmly, breaking down any resistance from hinges or latch. Fire resistant doors, where required, will also be there to keep smoke from entering the escape route and must therefore fit snugly against stops of adequate thickness.

ESCAPE ROUTES. G.L.C. The following house types will require fire protection and means of escape in the G.L.C. area as set out below, all examples being for multiple occupation. As all examples will depend on particular circumstances applicants are advised to discuss their projects with the Council's officers before making a formal application.

1 Two-storey house
With one occupation (i.e. dwelling) per storey, the fire risk would be low and special requirements unlikely. If the upper storey contains more than one dwelling, it should be divided by fire-resisting construction and the staircase enclosure and doors should have a reasonable standard of fire-resistance.

2 Two-storey house with basement
a The protection of the ground and first floors should be as in 1 above. The ground floor should be separated from the basement by fire-resisting partitions and a door, and the stair soffite from the ground to the first floor should be protected by plaster, plasterboard or asbestos wallboard.
b Where open basement areas adjoin the building or where the ground level is well below the ground floor level, the house becomes virtually a three storey building with escape from the middle floor. In this case the staircase should be separated from the living accommodation on the ground floor by fire-resisting partitions and fire-resisting self-closing doors, with the basement being cut off as in **a** above if it is not a separate dwelling with its own entrance at basement level.

3 Three or four-storey house with or without basement, with upward and downward escapes from the upper floors
Where a secondary (i.e. alternative) exit is possible, the following conditions should be met.
a A secondary exit to the roof and thence to the roof of an adjoining building or some other appropriate secondary exit from the upper part of the building to an adjoining building should be provided and made available at all times
b A fire-resisting screen and door between the stairs and the top-floor landing, to protect the landing, should be provided if the secondary exit is from that landing. Should the secondary exit be from a room or en-closed space, the screen and door need not be provided but the door and partition to the room or enclosed space should be fire-resisting and any added protection that might be necessary should be provided on the

staircase side. The door should not be locked and should be marked 'Fire Exit'

c The staircase enclosure and exit passage to the street should be protected and all doors therein except on the top storey be made fire-resisting and self-closing, protection being on the room side

d Any basement stairs from the ground floor should be separated from it by a fire-resisting door and spandril partition

e Different dwellings on any one floor should be separated by fire-resisting construction

4 Three-storey house with or without basement, with downward escape only from the upper floors

Where a secondary exit is not possible from the upper part, a staircase protected throughout, with separation from the basement, may be accepted provided the building excluding the basement does not contain more than 12 persons in not more than six flats. Where such a downward escape only is practicable the doors to the staircase in the top storey should be protected on the staircase side and the ceiling of the staircase should be protected on the underside against penetration of fire from the top of the staircase into the roofspace.

5 Three or four-storey house with or without basement with downward escape only from the upper floors

In houses of three storeys (other than in **4** above) or four storeys above pavement, where exit is from the upper storeys, only by way of the internal staircase, the following conditions should be met together with **3c** and **3d** above.

a The staircase, doors and exit way to the street should be similarly treated

b Where practicable the entrance to each floor from the protected staircase, except in the top and basement floors, should be through a lobby and, where the lobby is common to two or more flats, the lobby partitions and doors should be fire-resisting and the latter self-closing

6 House of five or more storeys with or without basement

a A secondary exit should be provided from the storeys above the fourth storey and a fire-resisting screen and door placed across the stairs at that level. The staircase and doors should be protected in all storeys and the requirements of **3a**, **3c** and **3d** followed

b Where a secondary exit either via the roof or by external staircase cannot be provided, lobby access on all floors other than the top and basement floors may be accepted to give a protected downward escape

Secondary exits

These may be by trap door or skylight easily openable without the use of a key. A dormer door or window or opening sash, also without a key, will suffice. Ladders should be of light but rigid construction with flat treads and should be permanently fixed at an approximate angle of 60 degrees. Where hinged they should be easily lowered by rope or pulley. Once out on the roof, the escaper should be provided with walkways of duckboards, fixed steps, ladders with flat treads and safeguarded by handrails so that safe escape can be made to the next building. It is well to bear in mind that the escaper may be an elderly person, unfamiliar with the roof, and trying to find his or her way in the dark

8 Underground Room Regulations

Basement floors in London, and some floors that one might consider to be ground floors, are controlled by Underground Room Regulations. These govern in a general manner the dampness in walls and floors, as well as the condition of the drainage, and ventilation and light to the rooms. These regulations usually impinge most on the size and light gained from the windows, which often have to be enlarged in a London terrace house where basement windows look into a narrow yard at the front or rear of the house. Light to these is measured above a 30 degree cut-off line to a solid obstruction within 10 ft (3.048 m). Therefore, say, forming glazed french doors to replace a window will not necessarily help as the extra glass at the bottom of the doors will be below the 30 degree cut-off line. If the existing window does not comply, it will probably need to be enlarged sideways or upwards to gain the additional light required.

Here is a typical Borough's list of regulations:

Regulations in Respect of Underground Rooms

REGULATIONS prescribed by the Mayor, Aldermen and Councillors of the London Borough of .... for securing the proper ventilation and lighting of rooms to which sub-section (2) of section 18 of the Housing Act, 1957, applies, and the protection thereof against dampness, effluvia or exhalation.

Every room used, or suitable for use for human habitation, the surface of the floor of which is more than three feet below the surface of the part of the street adjoining or nearest to the room, or more than three feet below the surface of any ground within nine feet of the room, shall comply with the following regulations, that is to say:—

DRAINAGE

1 The subsoil of the site of the room shall be effectually drained wherever the dampness of the site renders this necessary.

2 No subsoil drain shall discharge into a soil drain except through a suitable trap.

3 Every drain passing through the room, and every drain or sewer passing under the room, other than a subsoil drain, shall be gastight and watertight.

FLOORS

4 The floors of the room shall be of such material or materials and con-

struction as adequately to resist the passage of moisture or exhalation from the ground.

WALLS

5 The walls of the room shall either be of such material and construction or shall have been so treated, as adequately to resist the passage of moisture to their inner surface, or to any timber or other material forming part of the building that would be harmfully affected by dampness.

VENTILATION AND LIGHTING

6 The room shall have a window or windows as specified in paragraph (i) of this regulation for the purposes of ventilation, and in paragraph (ii) for the purposes of lighting.

(i) One or more windows which can be opened at the top directly into external air to an extent equivalent in aggregate area to not less than one-twentieth of the area of the floor of the room.

(ii) One or more windows having an aggregate area clear of the window frame amounting to not less than one-tenth of the area of the floor of the room, and so situated that from any point thereon, or if the total window area exceeds the foregoing minimum requirement, from any point on a part or parts thereof which satisfy that requirement, a line can be drawn upwards at an angle of thirty degrees with the horizontal in a vertical plane at right angles to the plane of the window without intercepting any obstruction except an open fence within a distance of ten feet measured horizontally from the window. For this purpose a bay window with side lights shall be deemed to be a flat window equal in area to the sum of the areas of the front and side lights, situated at a distance from the face of the wall from which it projects equal to half the maximum depth of the projection.

7 Immediately outside any window provided in pursuance of these regulations there shall be an unobstructed space which shall conform with the following requirements:—

a The space shall extend throughout the entire width of the window and (except where the area of such window is not less than one-seventh of the area of the floor of the room) for two feet on each side of the window.

b The space shall in every part extend for not less than two feet from the external wall of the room except that, where the window is a bay window with side lights, the depth of the space in front of the window may be reduced to not less than one foot.

c If the space is below the general level of the ground within nine feet from the window so much of it as satisfies the foregoing requirements of this regulation shall be properly paved with impervious material and effectually drained, and the paved surface shall be at least six inches below the level of the bottom of the sill of the window.

d Nothing in this regulation shall prohibit the placing in or over such open space of any steps necessary for access to any part of the building in which the room is contained provided they are not placed over or across any window or windows satisfying the requirements of the preceding regulations.

Town Clerk.

9 Preliminary Survey of the Building

Generally

This section deals with the inspection of the building to be converted, extended or altered with a view to ascertaining its structural state, the condition of finishes, evidence of wet rot, dry rot and insect infestation. Apart from the design and construction of particular alterations, the general condition of the building is always of importance and part of the contract for the building work may include items of maintenance and repair. The local authority, if it awards a grant for the work, may, as a condition for the grant, insist that the whole building is in a reasonable state to give it a life of 30 years. This will involve basic repairs, and, if the grant money is all used up in, say, expensive repairs and improvements to the basement, the remainder of the house must be brought up to a reasonable standard, whether subsidised by grant or not. Note that under the heading 'Action' various alternatives are suggested that may be selected depending on standard required or cost.

ROOFS   **Defects**

1 Broken pots, cracked haunchings, stack cappings broken
2 Cracked renderings to parapets, party walls above roof line
3 Old lead gutters, flashings
4 Roof finish: cracked, laminated or missing slates or tiles
5 Flat roof: cracked, blistered felt and asphalt
6 Flat roof: split or worn out metal roofing
7 Thatch: soggy and shapeless, slipping
8 Cedar shingles: rotting, splitting, fungus affected
9 Asbestos slates: discoloured, moss-covered, split

Action

1 Replace pots with new, or remove and cap flues to maintain ventilation with ridge tiles or asbestos ventilators. Alternatively add air bricks in side of stack and fit concrete or other slab over top. (Flues should be ventilated top and bottom when redundant, with rain penetration prevented)
2 Cut away defective renderings and re-render, or cut out cracks and make good. Bed down copings, make good joints between. Replace rendered copings with superior alternative (precast concrete coping stones, tiles, metal flashings etc.). Add d.p.c.s where appropriate.
3 If not repairable, strip off and relay in new lead or alternative. Check

substructure for rot etc. and repair or treat as necessary. Check for re-constructing substructure to alter or improve falls to outlets. Treat substructure against insect or rot attack before replacing lead or alternative. Cut chases in brickwork to take lead and make good after tucking in. Possibly replace defective lead stepped flashings with zinc, copper or felt

4 Replace individual slates and fix in place with zinc or lead clips. It is likely that this operation will itself dislodge other slates and the finished job can only be a temporary repair until the whole roof is properly re-laid.

Strip off slates, save those that can be re-used (not as high a percentage as may be hoped) and relay with second-hand to match. At same time decide whether battens need replacing, or strip off slates and battens, check and treat joists with preservative. Strengthen roof structure, purlins, ridge, struts, etc., if necessary. Examine wall plates for rot, size and fixing. If slates and battens are to be relaid, consider adding insulation blanket and roofing felt over joists if not existing. Check ridge tiles and rebed or repoint. Check vent pipes through roof, hatch flashings, dormer flashings. Where re-slating or re-tiling whole roof, consider using recovered slates or tiles on whole slopes, new or second hand on separate other slopes, so that differences in appearance are less obvious

5 Repair asphalt or strip and relay. Relay sheathing felt. Check over outlets, upstands. Blistered felt best removed and relayed owing to low cost against expense of temporary repair. Check substructure

6 Repair lead faults by 'burning'. Check for thickness and brittleness due to age. Similarly for zinc. Check cappings and possibility of rotten substructure. Consider temporary repairs against refitting with new metal. Consider other possibilities such as removing roof and fitting corrugated perspex for top lighting

7 Reed and straw thatch can be repaired. Sedge on ridges normally needs renewing every 20 years together with the wire netting if any. Reed will probably have to be totally renewed after 50–75 years (straw has a shorter life) but if the surface is damaged or affected by mould, in a shorter time, by cleaning and raking out loose reeds, washing off mould with fungicide. Then a 9 inch (225 mm) layer is laid over the top of the old, fixed to the old reed, with care taken to avoid slipping of the old. Wire netting must always be removed rather than left and covered over. Repair of straw thatched roofs is basically similar to reed, but likely to be necessary more often, a straw roof having a life of 20–30 years

8 Cedar shingles are laid with four thicknesses at one point. Although cedar resists decay, a shingle roof is subject to fungus growing and to general deterioration over the years. Also insects are attracted and shelter underneath. Woodpeckers can find this a good source for nourishment.

Cedar shingle roofs can be treated with a light grade of creosote to increase weathering and prevent onset of decay; treatment is repeated every five years. New shingles can be obtained with pressure impregnation. They are fixed with flat-headed copper, aluminium alloy or zinc-coated wire nails. I.C.I. 'Everdur' nails can be used for impregnated shingles

9 Asbestos slates can still be obtained for repairing old roofs, although the colour variation would be noticeable, owing to the new coloured asbestos

slates having a vogue. Cost of stripping old asbestos and replacing with new should be considered

ROOF STRUCTURE, ATTIC SPACE

Defects

Deflecting roof members, rot and insect attack, lack of insulation, inadequate tank supports, bad alterations in the past, inadequate roof hatch, i.e. too small for new larger tanks possibly required. Internal open gutters draining front parapet to rear. Bad brickwork to flues and side walls in attic space.

Action

Deflecting purlins should be replaced or strutted in some way, off a central partition or similar bearing point. If roof is being refinished, the support structure should be built when roof load is at its lowest. Rafters, collars and other timber members can be strengthened by bolting timbers alongside depending on the situation and importance of member, and presuming that it cannot be replaced adequately or satisfactorily. Areas where rot is possible are wall plates buried in damp walls, support timbers to leaking parapet or central valley gutters, leaking ridge tiles affecting ridge member, leaking side or stepped flashings affecting side joists or rafters, truss ends and bearings buried in damp walls, fascias to leaking external gutters, leaking rooflight frames. If roof space is to be used as habitable room, ceiling bearers will be inadequate and joists will be needed of sufficient size for floor loading. These can be laid between ceiling bearers or pinned alongside them, to make most of floor to ceiling height. Revise roof drainage, gutter outlets, etc., enclosing open gutters and changes to suit drainage required in other alterations in house.

Add insulation at 'floor' level or under rafters if to existing satisfactory roofing. If attic space is not to be made habitable, it is preferable to lay insulation over ceiling bearers to keep the volume of air to be warmed in the house to a minimum. When insulated in this way, the cold water and expansion tank if placed in the attic will have to be separately lagged (insulated) including any pipework that is above insulation at ceiling level. Ceiling bearer level insulation can be provided by fibreglass quilt, sheet polystyrene (or polyurethane), or loose mineral wool. Where insulation is to be fixed to the underside of the rafters, it must obviously be in sheet or quilt form for pinning to the roof structure. If the attic is to be inhabited, foil backed plasterboard could be used, with sheet or quilt insulation fitted between the rafters behind it. As insulation is cheap and easy to install, and because it is essential to conserve heat, it is more than ever important to provide it to a very good standard (see Appendix 3: table of insulation values).

For rot and insect attack see Chapter II.

Where the attic is to be used for storage, boarding or sheet material should be provided and carefully positioned over a partition or support other than mid-span ceiling joists. Form new hatch of adequate size for trunks or other bulky items to pass through. Consider use of loft ladder for easier access. There are many patent designs which are concealed above the hatch and drop down when the hatch is released. Check over brickwork to party walls in attic to make sure there are no holes into flues due to defective mortar, etc.

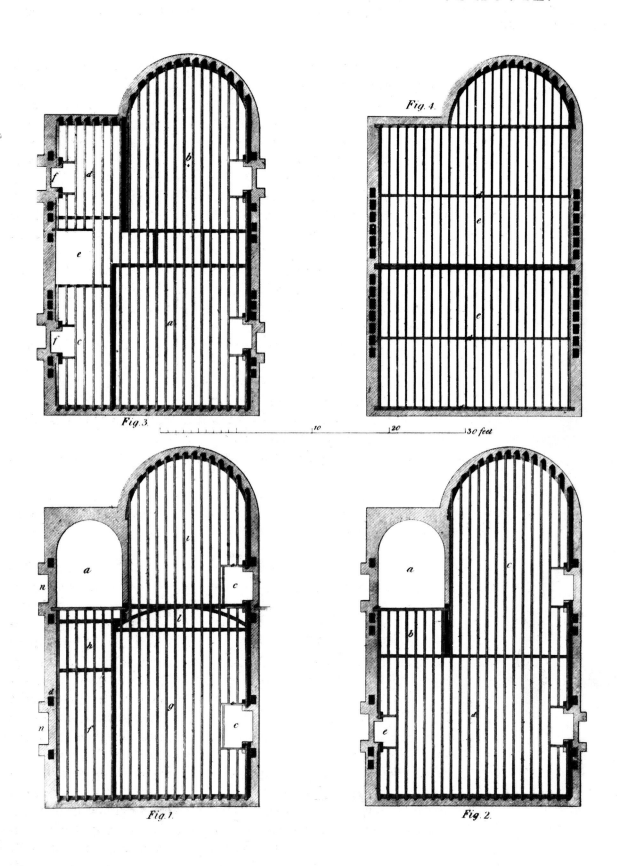

Fig. 4.

Fig. 3.

10   20   30 feet

Fig. 1.

Fig. 2.

46

FLOORS GENERALLY, EXCEPT BASEMENT OR GROUND FLOOR

Defects

Too much deflection, rot at joist ends, insect attack, low sound reduction.

Action

New joists can be bolted alongside existing, if floor is not to be rebuilt, with top to provide revised floor level when boarded. Where joist ends are rotten, they can be cut back to good wood and new joist length bolted on. Wall plate must be cut away and substituted after treatment of wall for rot. Remaining end of joist should also be treated. If wall plate is not replaced, its cavity should be bricked up and new joist ends hung on joist hangers built into wall. Ceiling plaster below will, of course, be destroyed and will need replacing where joists have to be cut back.

Where deflection in floor is acceptable, solid or herringbone bridging may be inserted to prevent joists twisting and to wedge the floor across the line of joists.

For insect and rot treatment see Chapter 11.

To provide better sound reduction through existing floors, a sound absorbent carpet will reduce impact noise (as will sheet floorings on under-layer of sponge rubber and cork).

To reduce airborne sound, the weight of the floor has to be increased. This can be done in various ways:

1 Increase thickness of plaster ceiling below
2 Adding pugging between the joists
3 Fitting battens above joists on absorbent quilt, to form 'floating' floor over existing, will reduce impact noise

See Chapter 13 for more details on sound insulation.

INTERNAL PARTITION WALLS

Defects

Bad alterations previously which may have weakened partitions, rot in posts to stud partitions, inadequate sizes of structure.

Action

If plaster is not defective, and no alterations are carried out to partitions it will not be apparent whether the posts, rails and noggings are adequate. However, if plaster has to be removed the true state of the partitions will be revealed and may then have to be dealt with. Inadequate timbers can be replaced and additional blocks, wedges, or noggings inserted. If timbers are affected by rot or insect attack (see Chapter 11), it may be advisable to cut away the whole partition to solve the problem, and reconstruct with treated timbers or replace with block or brickwork. Old stud partitions often have diagonal bracing members. Care should be taken when, say, building a new doorway that the diagonal bracing loads are transferred or taken up.

It should be noted that in many cases the central partitions parallel with the front wall of terrace houses will be carrying the floor joists and therefore be in compression. New openings should take this into consideration. Partition walls enclosing staircases normally support themselves only, with trimmers at landings bracing the staircase. In basements partition walls may be either stud and plaster, or brick, or a mixture in timber studs built into brickwork. This latter is bad construction and is usually affected by damp. As the brick is in panels between the studs, it is unstable. These

Plans of floor timbers in a 'first rate house'. This engraving taken from *The New Practical Builder and Workman's Companion* 1826, shows the layout of joists, trimmers and flues. The opening with semi-circular outside wall is for the staircase.

47

partitions are better taken down and rebuilt.

BASEMENTS AND
GROUND FLOORS

Defects

1 Damp, rot, insect infestation, bad floor construction, different floor levels, inadequate sub-floor ventilation
2 Inadequate-sized windows

Action

1 Rotten flooring and joists can be replaced with hardcore concrete and DPM etc. Local authorities usually insist on concrete but may allow new joists and flooring as long as there is a DPC and adequate airbricks for good ventilation below the floor. If a grant is to be paid, concrete will almost certainly be insisted on by local authority.

Damp-proofing will be required to walls showing signs of damp, or proved damp by means of a damp meter. (See Chapter 10 for damp-proofing remedies.) Changes of level in basements or ground floors usually found because of previous replacement of old rotten floors. Floors can usually be made the same level if desired where some are to be replaced. Existing brick or stone floors, if required to be kept but damp-proofed can be picked up and relaid on concrete and DPM. It will be found that some apparently concrete screeded but uneven floors are not properly laid down being of an inadequate thickness and strength.

2 Check window sizes (so often undersized in basements) for size and openings in relation to floor areas lit. Special regulations apply in London for angles of light from 'underground rooms' (see Chapter 8 for underground rooms' regulations), but building by-laws will also apply, of course.

EXTERNALLY: WALLS

Defects

1 Leaking or broken rainwater pipes, gutters, hoppers, outlets etc.
2 Brickwork bulging, bowing
3 Defective pointing
4 Deflecting lintels, arched lintels deteriorating
5 Brickwork cracks
6 Broken, cracked or rotten window sills
7 Stucco or rendered wall cracks
8 Old wall ties

Action

1 Green mould on brickwork behind RWPs will sometimes give a clue to cracked or leaking pipes. Cracks often occur behind the pipe and cannot be seen unless carefully examined. Gutters, apart from corroding, sag down and get out of their correct fall due to leaves and deposits weighing them down. Apart from minor repairs, probably better to scrap and re-organise and replace rainwater drainage. Eaves also tend to settle or change, and thus gutters on them deteriorate. Gutter boards behind defective gutters tend to rot and may need replacing, best done at same time as gutter
2 Brickwork which bows out or bulges can be rebuilt. The extent of the deformation and the cause should be investigated. The Building or District Surveyor may insist on rebuilding depending on measurement and

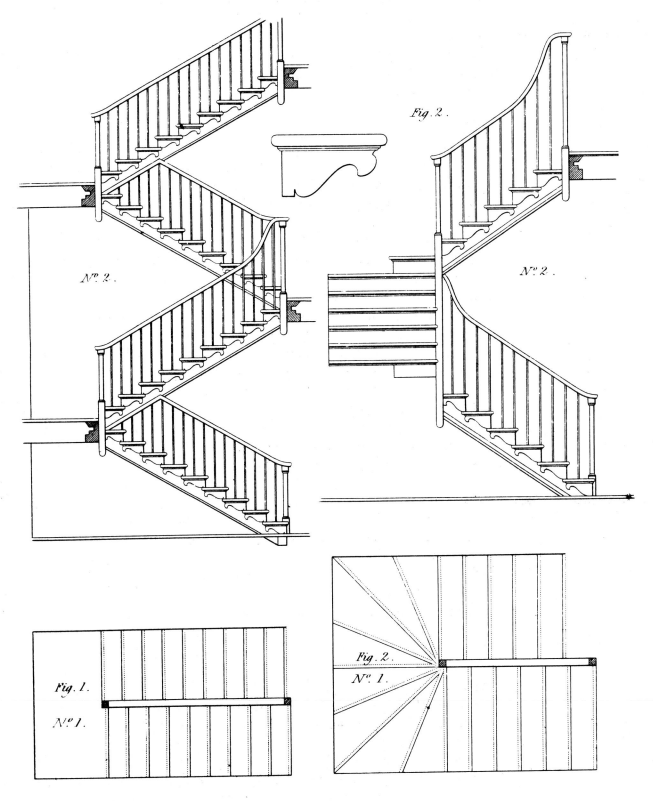

Fig. 2.

Nº. 2.

Nº. 2.

Fig. 1.

Nº. 1.

Fig. 2.

Nº. 1.

London, Published by Thoˢ Kelly, 17 Paternoster Row, Janʳ 2.1826.

E.Turrell sc.

A stair detail from *The New Practical Builder and Workman's Companion* showing the subtlety of the junctions, handrails and mouldings.

whether extra loads may be imposed on it due to alterations. Extensive rebuilding, such as a whole side wall, will probably bring problems of marrying new brick courses to old at corners and by building the new wall plumb, other walls out of plumb will be shown up and may cause bricklaying problems when bonding in courses

3 Pointing of mortar joints in old brickwork is often necessary, usually to those areas of brickwork most exposed to the weather such as the tops of walls near parapets, and on corners. Old mortar should be raked out to a depth of about $\frac{3}{4}$ in (20 mm) and repointed with new mortar, which can be coloured if necessary to match existing pointing

4 Defective lintels. Brick arches if showing fractures or misplacement can be taken down and rebuilt fairly simply, but depending on amount of fracture and whether it spreads into surrounding brickwork, when the underlying cause must be ascertained

5 Brickwork cracks. The reason should be deduced, but will most likely be found to be settlement in part of a foundation, possibly at a corner. Cracks are often found where, say, a porch or outbuilding abuts the main building, where differential settlement has occurred. The direction and extent of the cracks will indicate the cause. The cracks can usually be eradicated by toothing in new (or re-used) bricks in the cracked area right through the wall once it has been ascertained whether the cause of the crack is settlement and if so whether it is to be cured by underpinning if the settlement is still taking place, or whether all settlement has run its course

6 Window sills (stone, brick, concrete, etc.). Apart from the timber sill, the sub-sill may well be broken, cracked, or with its top surface being too flat. This latter is a common fault in old buildings, causing rot to the timber sill. Sills can be replaced, rebuilt, re-rendered, flashed, tiled, etc. The treatment should relate to the timber window sill and provide a good run-off for rain water

7 'Stucco' or rendered wall cracks. These cracks are not always due to settlement, although they will of course occur if this has taken place and cracked the wall behind. It is more likely to be the result of the wrong mix of render or chemical attack from the brickwork and mortar behind the finishing render. Depending on area involved and money available, hack off and re-render or cut out cracks, loose render and make good

8 Old wall ties. Although used very often in the past to restrain walls that appeared to be moving, wall ties with their end plates or frames cannot be entirely satisfactory. Corrosion can take place, and in brickwork, the sheer stress of the end plate horizontally can only actually restrain the brickwork covered by the plate. Sometimes the ties at, say first and second floors, are linked by a steel channel or other section. The real cause of the wall deformation should be deduced. The ties to the plates are sometimes taken horizontally right through the house to another plate on the other side. In the case of semi-detached houses an agreement should be reached with the adjoining owner for the removal of any ties. The rod can be cut off at the party wall and another plate fitted, possibly with wedges to induce tension. Note that wall tie bars will be within the floor thickness. Sometimes ties are taken some way into the building and bolted to trimmers which are strutted back to a wall to provide rigidity

EXTERNALLY: WINDOWS

Defects

1 Rotten sills, frames
2 Out of balance sashes
3 Broken glazing bars, glass

Action

1 Although sills can be 'faced up' with hardwood which can be done without removing the whole sill, it is obviously better to fit a new sill if possible. If so an improved section with steeper water run-off might be possible. A common fault in old wood sills is opening out of the wood grain leading to a fibrous condition which breaks down and rots in due course. No amount of filling and painting is likely to last very long on such an unsuitable surface open to the weather. The feet of side frames resting on and morticed into the sill is the most likely part to deteriorate where water has seeped or percolated into the end grain. Although this rotten timber can be cut away and pieced in, it may be better to fit a new window depending on money available and the condition of the window generally

2 Out of balance sash windows can usually be easily adjusted after fitting new cords, pulleys or other items causing friction or blockage. Weights can be reduced or increased to suit

3 Broken glazing bars and glass can be repaired and similar sections fitted to match other windows. Often it will be found that glazing bars have withered away and are held in position by the glass itself. One disappointment often met with is the decoration of old glazing bars and putty. This is often irregular and looks imprecise. However it is difficult to cut back old putty to a neat line as it has probably become brittle. If clean lines are essential, the glass should be taken out and rebedded. This however will almost certainly reveal defective glazing bars. You will probably have to decide either to leave well alone or renew

EXTERNALLY: DRAINAGE PIPEWORK, ABOVE AND BELOW GROUND

Defects

1 Corroded, broken pipework and fittings
2 Inadequate design, over design
3 Inadequate falls below ground
4 Leaks and testing below ground

Action

1 With corroded and defective pipes, it is probably better to scrap and refit new similar or PVC pipes. Pipe runs are often re-organised during alterations in any case to provide additional bathrooms, etc. Old lead pipes are now seldom satisfactory, and will not stand up to test, apart from being deformed and showing evidence of frequent repair

2 Existing pipework will have probably been built to old principles, festooned with anti-syphon and venting branches and of inadequate 'weight' of cast iron. With the new single stack systems and generally neater PVC design of fittings, it is an improvement aesthetically as well as functionally to redesign old pipework

3 If inadequate falls are found in underground drainage, this may be due to settlement of part of the drain run. Little can be done except to relay the drain, unless the drainage can be redesigned to eliminate or shorten

the affected length of drain

4 Leaks and defects to drains must be dealt with before seepage affects the ground below the house, possibly even the foundations, apart from the dangers to health. Underground drains can be tested by means of water or air. Where possible testing should be carried out from manhole to manhole, and short branches to a main drain between manholes included in the test for the main drain. Manholes are tested separately. During a water test, with a trap at the upper end of the line, a rubber tube should be passed through the trap to draw off trapped air. The drains are plugged with special plugs and then filled with water with a vertical pipe jointed at the top end temporarily to give a 5 ft (1.524 m) head of water. Subsidence of the test water will indicate that

a absorption is taking place in pipes and joints, or

b pipes and joints are sweating, or

c leakage is taking place at joints or pipes, or

d air is trapped somewhere in the system

If the water level drops a little, this will probably be due to absorption and should be topped up. An hour should be enough for a test.

Testing by air involves plugging the drain as before, and pumping air in to give a reading of 4 in (100 mm) of water indicated in a glass 'U' tube. Water should not fall below 3 in (76 mm) in a five minute period. Drain plugs should if possible be immersed in water to assist detection if the plugs are leaking air.

Testing by means of smoke for drains above ground involves the insertion of a smoke bomb in the drain pipe after sealing up the other ends. Smoke will emerge from any faults

EXTERNALLY: VAULTS, YARDS, GARDEN WALLS

Defects

1 Damp vaults

2 Yards with wrong levels, inadequate drainage, defective paving

3 Garden walls, leaning, collapsing, incomplete

Action

1 Improved damp-proofing renders and additives are becoming more reliable so that old coal vaults and basement entrances below entrance porches to first floors can be made waterproof at some expense. Coal vaults will be underground except for the yard side and may well still have the old coal hole in the pavement above. If the pavement paving is defective rain water will be penetrating. The local authority may be persuaded to repair or relay dangerous paving. The floors of vaults are often brick and will need to be relaid or concreted if vaults are to be properly damp-proofed for whatever use is intended

2 The level of yards can have an adverse effect on damp-proofing to the house wall. Settlement may have caused reverse falls from a yard gulley if any. You may have to reduce the general yard level to help with damp-proofing to main wall. Revised drainage may affect levels

3 Garden walls, if any, may require attention (see Chapter 7 for garden 'fence' walls). Piers to brick walls may exist and if on owner's side of wall, may indicate that the wall is in his ownership. Otherwise repairs to party or any dividing walls are best discussed with neighbours.

Foundations will probably be inadequate. If decision is taken to rebuild, this will also involve new foundations

DOORS GENERALLY, INCLUDING ARCHITRAVES

Defects

1 Warped, 'in wind'
2 Patched, morticed
3 Defective ironmongery
4 Split panels
5 Inadequate carpet clearance

Action

1 Although a warped door can be rehung to reduce the disagreeable appearance and lack of sound reduction through a bad fit, there is little that can be done to straighten it without considerable rebuilding which may not be worth while

2 Old doors often show signs of different locks and handles having been fitted during their life. Usually old mortices and patches can be pieced-in and, when rubbed down before decoration, leave a reasonable looking door on completion. But the cost of repairs to doors, frames and architraves should be assessed as it might be cheaper to fit new ones. Take into consideration also the cost of burning off old paint and clearing out mouldings to architraves and door panels if any, against replacing with new

3 Old ironmongery has special attractions, but may be defective. Keys can be made for old locks, but it may be decided to renew all ironmongery. Hinges on old doors may be split across their screw holes, and should be replaced

4 Split panels in panelled doors cannot often be hidden by filling and making good by the decorator. If painted, it is better to replace the panel. If hardwood it may not be easy to match, and therefore better to leave and make good, depending on the decorator's skill

5 If carpets are to be used, doors may have to be taken off and reduced at the bottom to clear carpet thickness. It is better to foresee this problem before the carpet layers arrive

ELECTRICAL INSTALLATION

Defects

1 Old wiring and equipment
2 Insufficient cable size for increased load
3 Insufficient earthing
4 Current leakage shown by test
5 Unsuitable layout of wiring

Action

1 The date of an installation can usually be deduced from the design of switches, look of the wiring, and its type. Old rubber-clad wiring may now be defective and if extra points have been fitted since first installed, overloaded

2 Alterations usually imply a heavier loading with more electrical equipment being installed. Existing wiring will get overloaded, new circuits at least will have to be run. Check with electricity board whether supply cable is adequate for increased load

3 Overhead cables supplying houses should have earth leakage trip mechanisms. Earthing is often inadequate on existing installations where the supply is overhead

4 Wiring can be tested by means of a Megger which can detect current leakage out of a wiring installation

5 Where a house is to be divided into flats, separate meters will involve considerable rewiring and reorganisation to all parts of the electrical layout. Incoming supply cables can be cut back in length, or repositioned if not lengthened. To extend the cable it will be necessary to renew it with a longer length, rather than make a joint

WATER PIPEWORK, TANKS

Defects

1 Old pipes
2 Inadequate sized pipes
3 Rusty tanks
4 Mixed metals

Action

1 Old lead pipes can be kept but a decision is needed as to state, size or number of past repairs, condition of stop cocks, etc

2 Water pressures may have changed from original installation to time of alteration and pipes should be increased or decreased to suit if necessary. Water board should be consulted if increased service pipe size is required

3 Rusty galvanised tanks can be assessed as to likely life span left. Although tanks can be cleaned out and painted with a non-toxic bituminous composition to BS 3416 1961, it will probably be better to replace with a new tank if other pipe connections are proposed

4 Different metals are sometimes found where, say, copper pipes have been connected direct to a galvanised tank. Mixtures of different metals in a water pipework system may result in corrosion by electrolytic action. Metals should be separated by inert connectors. If not possible, a 'sacrificial anode' should be introduced into the tank, such as a lump of zinc or aluminium. This will have to be renewed from time to time

GAS PIPEWORK

Defects

1 Size of service pipe
2 Old installation

Action

1 Usually, if a gas central-heating system is to be installed, the existing service pipe will be of adequate size as it would have supplied old gas fires in most rooms. Gas Board will advise. If the house is being converted into flats with their own boilers, probable that new larger service pipe will be required, apart from running pipes to individual flats

2 An old installation with sub-floor pipes to fires, poker points, heater, cooker, etc. should be tested for corrosion and damage during construction period

10 Damp-proofing

Scope of this section

This section deals with remedial action necessary to cure damp in brickwork at ground floor and basement level. It does not cover problems with damp found in the upper parts of a building which are dealt with elsewhere under Chapter 9.

Generally

Anyone familiar with conversion work will be aware how many buildings were badly constructed in the past with little or no attention being paid to the prevention of rising damp. Whenever a central London house with a basement floor comes up for conversion it is almost certain to be obviously damp unless it has been treated already. Even if it appears to be in reasonable condition (possibly redecorated by the owner immediately before sale) a damp meter should be used to determine the latent damp held in the plaster or brickwork. If an Improvement Grant is being sought for the work, a damp meter test would almost certainly be applied by the local authority responsible to determine what work would be demanded by the authorities before a grant would be paid.

As most basement accommodation in London provided for the old kitchen range and the cook's accommodation, seldom visited by the owner, one must charitably presume that it was thought that the heat of the range, lit all the year round, would to some extent hold back the damp, or at least dry the resulting humid atmosphere.

BASEMENT FLOORING

1 Inspection

Whether the walls are damp or dry, the flooring should be examined. Usually a mixture of concrete in some areas (hall, scullery, vault under the porch, etc.) and timber floor boarding on joists will be found. If the joists, wall plates, and under floor ventilation through perimeter air bricks (and airways through partitions) are found to be free of rot, damp and the ventilation adequate, the local authority may allow it to remain.

2 Action

However, it is unlikely that timber basement flooring would be free of all these defects and the likely course will be to take out and cut away all floor and sub-floor timbers and replace them with a solid floor of concrete slab on hardcore, with a screed topping to receive the required floor finish. The damp proof membrane could be placed (a) under the concrete slab on top of blinded hardcore, (b) on the slab and under the screed, (c) at mid point in the slab itself, (d) on top of the screed itself in the form of an asphalt floor finish. In all cases it must link up with any new (or existing) d.p.c. in the walls, by being brought up the inside face of the walls to link with the horizontal d.p.c. in the walls (methods described below).

3 Factors affecting action

In any conversion it is probable that part of the basement or ground floor will have to be taken up in any case to:

a reconstruct drainage running under the floor, common in London

b make new drainage connection from, say, new soil stack for new bathrooms, new kitchen drainage, etc. with internal manholes, gullies, etc.

c where new walls internally or externally require foundations which will involve destruction of part or all of the adjacent existing flooring

d to provide new ducts for warm air heating, radiator pipework, gas or electricity service pipes and cables

e to effect reduction of floor level required by local authority to provide adequate floor to ceiling height to comply with regulations.

f where provision of an electric under-floor heating installation with wires buried in screed might involve a new concrete and screed floor if existing is timber, or revisions to an existing screeded or concrete floor to provide proper cover to the wires and sub-floor insulation as well as meeting the requirements for floor to ceiling heights

BASEMENT OR GROUND FLOOR DAMP PROOF FLOOR MEMBRANES

For the floor membrane, two types of material could be used: liquid applied and sheet.

Liquid applied

These are bituminous based materials and are applied by spray, mop or brush to the concrete surface in one or more coats, cold or hot. The manufacturer's instructions must of course be followed, and it is recommended that the local authority's approval be obtained for the use of a particular brand before putting in hand. The following manufacturers make products that may be suitable for application to the concrete slab surface.

Material and Manufacturer	Form in which used	Method of application
Bitastec (three grades) General Industrial Bitumens Ltd.	Black asphalt semi-liquid bitumen composition	Applied cold by brush
Bituseal Membranes Sealocrete Group Sales Ltd.	Liquid	Applied without primer by brush in 2 coats
Colset Bitumen Industries Ltd.	Emulsified bitumen in liquid or plastic form	Liquid applied by brush, plastic applied by trowel

Material and manufacturer	Form in which used	Method of application
Protective Coatings Shell Composites Ltd.	Stable bitumen emulsions and other compounds in various grades fibrated and unfibrated	Manufacturer's specifications to be followed
Mulseal Expandite Ltd.	Bitumen/rubber latex emulsion	Applied by spray, brush or squeegee with or without reinforcing membrane of fibreglass, hessian or scrim
Proofex Expandite Ltd.	A range of bitumen and bitumen/latex emulsions and solutions	Use of primer no. 6 required
D.P.C. Emulsion Expandite Ltd.	Bitumen/latex emulsion	Applied cold by brush or squeegee
D.P.C. Solution Expandite Ltd.	Bitumen solution with asbestos filler	Applied cold by brush or spray
Pallol Black Protective Coating Pallas Chemicals	Black bituminous	2 coats supplied ready for use, quick drying
Pudlo Bitumen Membrane Kerner-Greenwood	Bitumen/rubber emulsion	2 coat application, cold
Ritolastic Protective Coatings L.T.D. Building Products	Black coatings	Applied by brush or spray, cold
RIW Liquid Asphaltic Composition RIW Protective Products Ltd.	High grade asphaltic composition based on natural asphalt	2 coats applied cold by brush or spray
Setcrete II Cementation Chemicals Ltd.	Bitumen and rubber latex emulsion	2 coats applied with brush
Synthabar Thomas Ness Ltd. (National Coal Board)	Plasticised pitch product	Applied hot in one coat

Material and manufacturer	Form in which used	Method of application
Synthaprufe Thomas Ness Ltd. (National Coal Board)	Bituminous latex emulsion	Brush on cold to manufacturer's instructions
Heviprufe Thomas Ness Ltd. (National Coal Board)	Two-pack coal tar pitch/epoxy resin	Applied cold in one coat
Tektam Chemical Building Products Ltd.	Liquid and plastic bituminous asbestos fibre compositions	Brush or trowel applied
Tretol 202T/200T DPC System Tretol Building Products Ltd.	Pure bitumen solutions	Applied cold in two coats
Tretolastex Tretol Building Products Ltd.	Pure bitumen rubber solution	Applied cold two or three coats
Tretolastex Damp Surfaces Primer Tretol Building Products Ltd.	Pure bitumen rubber solution in hydro carbon solvents with special additives	Used as primer in damp conditions
Tretoflex Tretol Building Products Ltd.	Blended coal tar/resin two part, cold mixed	Trowel and airless spray application, on manufacturer's advice
Ventrot Plycol-Montgomerie Ltd.	Bituminous compound	Applied hot to manu- facturer's instructions

There are many other products similar to the above.

Sheet damp-proof membranes

The following products and manufacturers can provide polythene sheet d.p.m. materials. Thickness recommended 1000 gauge (250 microns).

Material and manufacturer		
BCL Blanket Dampcourse British Cellophane Ltd.	Supplied in roll form in widths 2 m (100 m long), 4 m (50 m long) and 8 m (25 m long)	

Material and manufacturer	
Tensiltarp Polythene Tarpaulin British Cellophane Ltd.	Available 6.4 m and 7.32 m widths, 19 m long, thickness 0.375 mm
Latcothene A. Latter & Co. Ltd.	Polyethylene film available in thickness 38, 65, 125, 250 microns, and widths 1.2 m, 1.5 m, 2.0 m, 4.0 m. Translucent, but some widths and thicknesses black
Marleythene Film The Marley Tile Co. Ltd.	Thicknesses 38, 65, 125 and 250 microns, widths 1.2 m, 2.0 m and 4 m, lengths 25 m, 50 m and 100 m
Ruberfilm Damp-proof Membrane Ruberoid Building Products Ltd.	A heavy duty polyethylene sheet of 300 microns (1200 gauge). Rolls 25 m by 4 m wide. Ruberstrip adhesive tape should be used to seal the laps
Visqueen British Visqueen Ltd.	Polythene building sheet is made in 4 ft (1.21 m), 6 ft (1.82 m), 12 ft (3.65 m) and 24 ft (7.31 m) rolls in the following thicknesses: 0.0015, 0.0025, 0.005 and 0.010 in

Plastic membranes other than polythene, or a combination of polythene and other material

Material and manufacturer	Form in which used
Bitu-thene Servicised Division of W. R. Grace Ltd.	A preformed flexible self-adhesive bitumen/polythene d.p.m. supplied in rolls 36 in (914 mm) wide, 60 ft (18.28 m) long.
No. 5 Pluvex Bitumen Sheeting Ruberoid Building Products Ltd.	A flexible sheeting reinforced with a strong base of fully saturated closely woven hessian. Applied in two layers welded together by blow lamp after adhesion of first layer to concrete, which should be primed with Ruberoid primer

There are many other sheet membrane materials available.

DAMP-PROOFING OF BASEMENT AND GROUND FLOOR EXISTING WALLS

Many different situations exist in the relationship of basement or ground floors to the ground level externally. There is of course the conventional case of floor level being 6 in (152 mm) or so above the ground level and treatment for curing rising damp in the absence of any damp-proof course is fairly straightforward. However, where the ground level varies from the above situation to total burial of the room below ground, the treatment of such structures is complicated and expensive. In addition both situations can occur in one building on a hillside or with a front 'area' at one end and garden at ground floor level at the other.

Various methods are described and shown below for tackling the damp-proofing of walls in different situations.

Asphalt tanking

Perhaps the best method for some situations, but also possibly the most expensive, asphalt tanking if applied externally would involve the excavation of earth in the area to be tanked sufficient for the manual application of the asphalt by the asphalters. The asphalt would have to be taken down the exterior face of the wall to a sufficient depth to link with a horizontal d.p.c. through the external wall linked with the floor d.p.m. inside. The asphalt should be 3 coat work, to finish not less than 20 mm in thickness. Each coat should lap 75 mm on vertical work. There should be a 2 coat asphalt fillet at all internal angles. As soon as possible, the asphalt should be protected by the erection of a brick or block skin wall, which should be built clear of the tanking by, say, 1 in (25 mm), and flushed up course by course to ground level. The asphalt tanking would be carried up to form a 'skirting' above ground level 6 in (152 mm) minimum and tucked into a splayed groove cut in the walling. The excavation can then be back-filled to the required ground level.

Asphalt tanking can also be applied internally. This method would save on external excavation, which might be in rock, or involve excavating concrete pavings or a road or pathway. However, it would involve loss of interior floor area as the asphalt tanking, all as described above for use externally, would have to be protected internally by a brick wall, a 'loading' wall of sufficient stability to withstand water pressure and prevent same pushing off or blowing the asphalt. Some special situations may suit this solution but its application is likely to be limited on grounds of cost and space wasting. Problems would also occur at timber door and window frames in the wall to be treated as they would remain in the damp wall and would require isolating from the damp.

Damp-course insertion

A damp course can be inserted in a wall to produce a similar d.p.c. to that which should have been provided in the first place. Brickwork can be cut away in sections and slate, bituminous felt, lead, zinc, copper or polythene inserted and the brickwork replaced. Alternatively, a mortar joint can be sawn through, mechanically or by hand, and a d.p.c. material such as one of the above fed into the saw cut. This work is also done in sections.

The thickness of the wall is a factor as can be imagined when hand sawing has to be undertaken. Mechanical sawing can be done if the equipment can be got near enough to the wall to be treated. With walls of varying thickness, some can be sawn and other parts may have to be treated by cutting away several courses in short lengths.

Among firms who carry out this type of d.p.c. work are:
Damp Coursing Ltd.
M.D.C. Group Services
Rentokil Discovac Damp-proofing (Rentokil Ltd.)

Damp-course by fluid injection

This is a comparatively recent method, which is not approved for instance by the London Borough of Kensington and Chelsea where work attracting grant aid may not be done by this method. Damp-proofing by injection usually is guaranteed for 20 years by the contractor installing the damp course. The system is based on the saturation of brickwork by silicone based fluids (or solutions with silicones) introduced into the brickwork either by a drip process or injection. In either case holes are drilled into the brickwork at centres approximating 6 in (152 mm) depending on the method or the contractor being used, and on the line of the d.p.c. required. It is claimed that the silicone solution permeates the surrounding brickwork and forms a barrier against rising damp. Generally this method is the one in most common use in the London area because of its flexibility in use (it is comparatively easy to inject brickwork in vaults, under staircases, etc.), the guarantees given, and the cost. Integral with this, and other methods, is the cost involved in the essential hacking off of plaster internally to a height at least 12 in (305 mm) above the highest damp reading before the injection operation is carried out, and the re-plastering of the treated wall afterwards to a special re-plastering specification recommended by the injection contractor.

Some firms that carry out damp-proofing by injection methods are given below. Some of them also carry out treatments for wood boring insects, wet and dry rot, etc.

Dampcoursing Ltd.	As well as carrying out d.p.c.s by the sawing and insertion method described above, this firm also do a d.p.c. system by chemical infusion, as well as providing a general service in water-proofing internal and external walls with special renders
Cambridge Timber-proofing Laboratories	Have a method of injecting under pressure a combination of water soluble siliconate and rubber latex, the Actane process. $\frac{3}{8}$ in (9 mm) diam. holes are drilled at $4\frac{1}{2}$ in (114 mm) centre to centre. This process can be used in some instances where there is hydrostatic pressure
Protim Knapen Gallwey Ltd.	This firm injects the chemical under pressure at low level and inserts porous clay syphon tubes into the wall above the injected d.p.c. at a slight upward angle at regular intervals to extract dampness from above the d.p.c. by forced evaporation. The firm also tackle woodworm and dry rot
London Woodworm & Dry Rot Controllers Ltd.	Inject their chemical d.p.c. as well as dealing with woodworm and dry rot problems
M.D.C. Group Services	Apart from their mechanically inserted d.p.c. mentioned above, they also do a chemically injected d.p.c. system

Nubold Ltd.	Offer a selection of fluids for chemical d.p.c. Nubex Standard (silicone based) is for pressure injection, Nubex 'W' (water-based siliconate) for the drip method. Site consultations are offered
Romanite D.P.C. No. 132 (L.T.D. Building Products)	Silicone-based aqueous solution for injection into brickwork, stone, etc., by drip feed or pressure injection
Peter Cox Ltd.	Employ a patented transfusion method by the drip method. A silicone based low viscosity liquid is transfused into the wall by apparatus designed to maintain absolute control of material so that an even distribution of the chemical is ensured throughout the full thickness of the fabric
Solignum Ltd.	This company offer silicone and siliconate fluids for drip or pressure injection
H. Tiffin & Son Ltd.	Carry out damp-proofing work by chemical injection as well as dealing with woodworm and dry rot. They also tackle damp with an electro-osmosis system. See later
Wykamit P.1. (Wykamol Ltd.)	A clear organic solvent silicone resin solution for pressure injection

Damp-courses provided by electrical means

The newest development in combating rising damp, electro-osmosis, is intended to eliminate the electrical potential difference between a damp wall and the soil in which it stands. Moisture movement ceases within the wall, which dries by evaporation.

Rentokil Electro-Osmotic Damp-proofing (Rentokil Ltd.)	A $\frac{3}{8}$ in (9 mm) wide copper strip is mortared into the damp wall at normal d.p.c. level and connected to a copper-clad earth rod driven between 12 and 20 feet (3.6 and 6.1 m) into the adjacent soil. Installation can take two days in a conventional house and on completion, the only visible evidence being a small bronze box on the wall. There is a 20-year guarantee. Rentokil Ltd. say they have done many thousands of installations in this way.
M.D.C. Group Services	Also have a system of damp-proofing by the electro-osmosis method.

There are many other firms who use this system.

Rendering and plastering in relation to damp-proofing work to ground floors and basements

1 If the walls to be treated for damp-proofing as outlined in sections above are already plastered internally, this plaster will show the signs of damp which drew attention to the lack of a d.p.c. in the first place, and will have to be hacked off at least 12 in (305 mm) beyond any point where a damp reading can be registered. Plaster is affected by damp over a long period and will not recover even if the source of the damp is cured.

If plaster is to be hacked off to, say, a height of 4 ft (1.2 m) above the floor level, the decision must be taken as to whether all the plaster be hacked off. The plaster, if old, may be loose or 'live' after the hacking work has been done and may have to come off anyway. In addition the plastering specification for the hacked off areas, to comply with requirements of the damp course contractor, may result in a thicker plaster cover than that existing above the four foot (1.2 m) line (or whatever height) which will therefore show a line where the plaster thicknesses vary. This new plasterwork can often be done by the damp course contractor as part of his contract and by his own plasterers, and covered by his guarantee. In case of breakdown of the remedial damp-proofing action, both facets of the operation (damp-course and plastering) would be under guarantee by the same contractor and blame more easily attached. Usually the re-plastering work is more cheaply done by the main contractor's plasterers, who will probably have other plastering work to do in the building at the same time. In the event of damp-proofing failure, it is not easy to decide whether it is the damp course or the re-plastering that has failed, with perhaps each party denying responsibility.

The insertion or injection of a d.p.c. usually takes place early in the contract, as demolition and hacking off of plaster is usually also involved. It is essential that the re-plastering of hacked-off plaster areas is delayed as long as possible to allow the damp brickwork to dry out. Basements that have been damp for many years must be given time to dry out, and both plastering and redecoration not carried out until each stage is dry, otherwise spoilt decorations will soon occur. The owner must be warned that there will be delays in occupancy where work to basements previously untreated is carried out and it is unwise to expect otherwise.

When damaged plaster is hacked off in old buildings, it will often be found that the brickwork is in a bad state and must be repaired before plastering can take place. Our predecessors often built extremely badly. Timbers are found built into brick partition walls at basement level. These will almost certainly be rotten and if found in a stud and brick partition construction, will possibly involve the rebuilding of the wall itself.

2 There are various water-proofing additives for use with renderings and concrete. The damp-proofing firms noted recommend special fluids for use in replastering walls after they have been injected or d.p.c.s. have been inserted.

The following are those brands of silicone water-proofers which:

a are tested and approved by BS 3826: 1969 and are licensed to carry the B.S.I. kite mark of quality:

Nubex and Nubindex (Nubold Ltd.).

b claim compliance with BS 3826: 1969 and its recommendation of a 5% silicones content:

Conservado 5 (Sika Ltd.)
Crodabuild 120 (Croda Polymers Ltd.)
Grangers 1210 Proofing (Grangersol Ltd.)
Hydralex (Associated Building Products Ltd.)
Hydrocide SX 5 per cent (Floor Life and Building Chemicals Ltd.)
Hydrol Hy-Sil Solution 29, 29F (with fungicide), 37 (Hydrol Ltd.)
Neocosal (Berk Ltd.)
Pudlo Silicones Waterproofer (Kerner Greenwood & Co.)
Repelicone S (Cementation Chemicals Ltd.)
Romanite W.R. (L.T.D. Building Products)
SBD Agnapel (SBD Construction Products Ltd.)
Synthasil (Coal Products Division, N.C.B.)
Szerelmey Silicone Liquid No. 103 (Szerelmey Ltd.)
Tretol Silicone Waterproofer (Tretol Ltd.)
Wykamit 'A' & 'W.R.' (Wykamol Ltd.)

11 Dry Rot, Wet Rot and Insect Attack

The house may well be affected by rot or insect attack and these must be discovered and dealt with.

DRY ROT (Merulius Lacrymans) Poor ventilation of under-floor timbers and rising damp are likely to be the cause of 'dry rot'. But damp infiltrating into the structure from, say, a porch or roof built against the main wall, and finding its way into an area of un-ventilated timber, can also cause this virulent fungus. The rot is detectable through a mushroomy smell and in appearance has a plate-like or bracket-like growth white-grey at the edges and rusty red at the centre. It can also produce hyphae or filament growths which grow over brickwork and penetrate plaster or soft mortar. They can carry water and will seek out other timber to attack such as skirtings, picture rails and door frames. Timber that is attacked will eventually show deep cracks and splits along and across the grain, so much so that pieces can be broken off and crushed between the

Large fruit body of dry rot fungus, Merulius Lacrymans, at the top of a doorway.

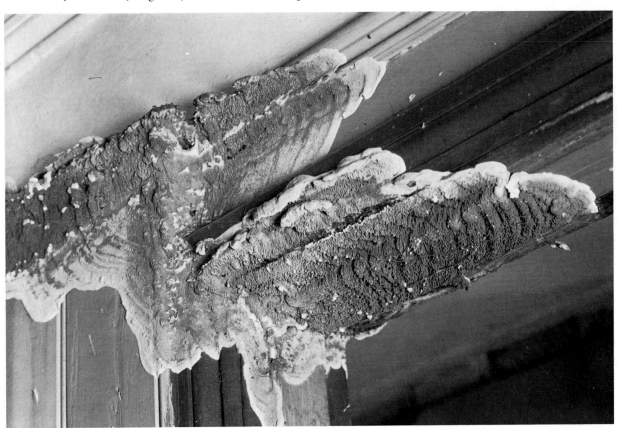

INS.

Cracking may appear similar for different fungi. The top example shows dry rot (*Merulius Lacrymans*), the bottom cellar fungus (*Coniophora Cerebella*).

fingers. The fungus will also spread itself with dustlike spores released into the air to seek out fresh fields to conquer.

To eradicate this fungus, every bit of it must be exterminated or it will break out again. At the same time the faulty construction which provided the conditions in the first place should be improved to prevent a recurrence of the attack. Specialist firms of course can deal with the treatment and eradication and usually give a guarantee. The work can be done by a competent builder in collaboration with architect or surveyor, but knowledge and experience are vital if it is not to be a waste of time. Anyone giving a guarantee is obviously likely to price highly for such a document, and to be safe will insist on considerable exploration work to discover the extent of the fungus. The cost of the treatment may well be less than the cost of replacement of plaster, rotten timber, or timber likely to have been infected.

66

Treatment

When affected material has been cut away, it should be immediately burnt to prevent spread of spores etc. This includes all sawdust, shavings and dust. In cutting away, it is usual to go at least 0.5 m beyond the point where dry rot can be seen to reach.

Fungicide should be applied to any fungus growth before cutting away to kill spores before they become airborne through disturbance. Fungicide is then applied to all affected areas including brickwork. Very thick walls should be drilled to allow the fungicide to be sprayed in under pressure.

Blow lamps can be used, but there is a risk that the fungus may still be lurking, whereas fungicide would linger on and deter any future outbreak.

WET ROT (Coniophora Cerebella)

Sometimes known as cellar fungus or cellar rot, wet rot needs timber with a moisture content of at least 25% and wet conditions in which to thrive. Although brownish in colour rather like some parts of dry rot, the timber tends to split mainly along the grain and not across it. The fruit body is like a thin green or brown sheet and produces spores and hyphae. However, it does not itself produce conditions for its better propagation and is not so virulent as dry rot.

Cellar fungus (*Coniophora Cerebella*) rotting a floor board. Note the cracks along the grain, and the dark strands. Compare also with the example on page 66.

Treatment

To eradicate wet rot, the affected wood should be cut away and burnt and the damp conditions eradicated. It is wise to treat the area with fungicide as a precaution against dry rot gaining a foothold in the same area.

**PORE FUNGUS
(Poria Vaillantii)** Rarer than wet and dry rot. It has strands spreading out rather like string, but timber tends to crack along and across the grain. Treatment as for wet rot.

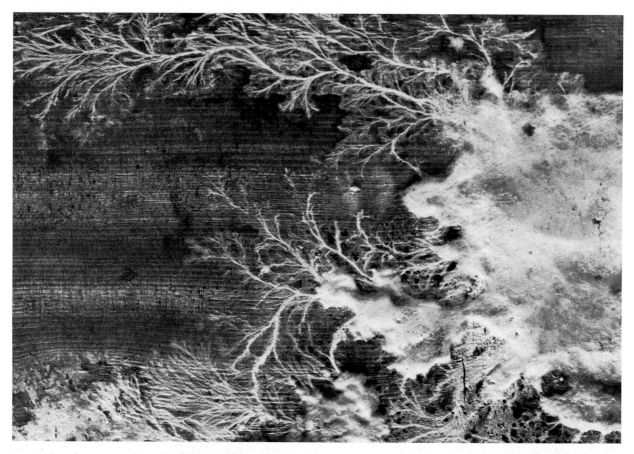

Poria Vaillantii, one of the wet rot fungi. Mycelium in form of sheets and strands shown on a board.

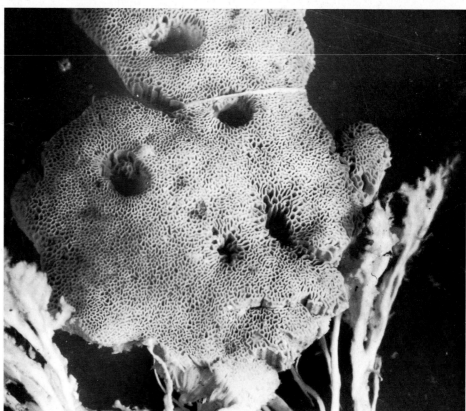

Poria Vaillantii, the fruit body.

FURNITURE BEETLE
(anobium punctatum) Found in soft and hardwood in a house structure as well as in furniture. It has a cycle of egg, larva, crysalis, and beetle, and it is in the larva stage that it tunnels and weakens timber to an extent depending on the number of beetle larva at work. The beetles emerge to mate about June, July or August.

Common furniture beetle attack in a pine floor board. The tunnels have been exposed by planing the surface.

Treatment

To eradicate the furniture beetle, the affected timber can be brushed, sprayed or injected with chemical insecticide after the timber has been cleaned down, and the roof space cleared out with vacuum cleaners. Insects can be attacked with gas, but the area to be treated has to be sealed off. Thorough treatment with spray or brush or injection is probably a safe method. New timber to be introduced into an affected area should be treated before it is incorporated.

Specialist firms carry out this work rather in the same way as dealing with damp or rot. The same firm will usually be able to do all this work, although sometimes different surveyors are sent from the same firm to investigate damp or insect damage. Guarantees will be given, but as can be imagined, it is 'quite something' to claim that a house has been cleared of beetles.

69

DEATHWATCH BEETLE (xestobium rufovillosum) Has a life cycle of 3 to 10 years and likes hardwood, especially the outer sapwood layers and timber affected by decay and fungus. Attack is usually more likely in damp areas such as wall plates, rafter feet and built-in timbers. The pupa emerge to mate in April, May and June. During this time the tapping sound can be heard which is the mating call. Softwood is rarely attacked. The grubs are larger than the furniture beetle grub and make larger and more extensive holes in the timber. Treatment is the same as for furniture beetle, i.e. spraying or injecting with insecticide.

Damage caused by death-watch beetle exposed at the centre of old structural timber.

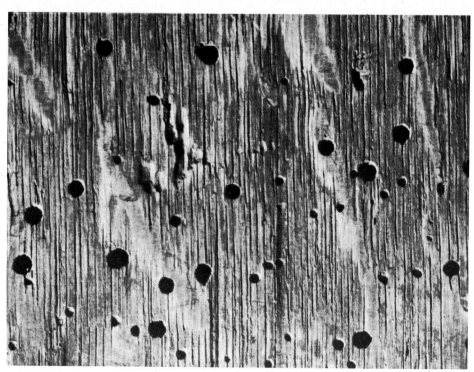

Flight holes of the common furniture beetle (1·5 mm) and death-watch beetle (3 mm) in same piece of timber. Approximate diameter of holes.

HOUSE LONGHORN
BEETLE
(hylotrupes bagulus)

Mostly confined to Surrey and likes timber less than 50 years old. It is a large beetle, leaves oval holes, and emerges in June or August. Treatment as for all beetle attack.

House long-horn beetle attack. The top photograph shows the situation before removal of surface skin which revealed severe structural damage.

PIN HOLE BORER   Attacks unseasoned hardwoods and is not therefore found often in buildings.

A piece of beech wood
under attack from pinhole
borer beetles (ambrosia
beetles).

12 Heating

At a time when the supply of energy for heating houses has been disrupted by industrial action or its cost raised by the suppliers and multiplied by inflation to a level unimagined in early 1973 (except by a few), it is not an easy task to advise on the selection and design of heating systems for the future; but perhaps the principal reasons for choosing one system over another for a given situation, for considering insulation, selecting a fuel and making other decisions are still the same, although requiring revaluation in the prevailing economic conditions. There has always been the development of equipment to keep pace with. The arrival of balanced-flue boilers had considerable bearing on designing conversions and later the development of another range of forced draught balanced-flue wall mounted units had further implications.

The rise in the cost of oil and coal is reflected in the rise of electricity charges, and even the cost of natural gas has risen, although not in the same proportion. The following table shows comparative costs of domestic fuels. It should be borne in mind that the efficiency of the equipment converting the fuel into heat is also a factor.

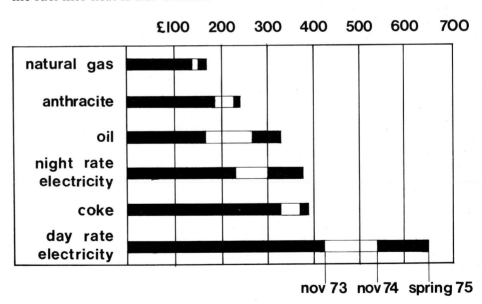

TABLE OF RELATIVE FUEL COSTS

An independent organisation, The National Heating Consultancy, of Gardner House, 188 Albany Street, London, NW1 4AP, produced figures in November, 1974, showing past, present and predicted fuel costs for different fuels. These figures represent the likely expenditure on the various fuels for a 1950 ft² (181 m²) three-bedroom detached house for temperature controlled central heating and hot water, and assuming loft insulation of 2 in (50.8 mm), a lagged hot water cylinder, but no other insulation. A heating load of 60–65,000 BTU was calculated to provide 70°F in living rooms, 65°F in utility rooms and 60°F in bedrooms for a 32-week heating season. Temperatures would be allowed to fall at night.

The figures given in the table do not include the standing charges.

The amounts of fuel considered as necessary to heat this house all as noted above were calculated as natural gas 2030 therms, anthracite 7.8 tons, oil 1331 gallons, night rate electricity 55518 units, coke 12.7 tons, day-rate electricity 41003 units.

It must be stated that the Electricity Council and National Coal Board dispute these figures. It should also be pointed out that this calculation is for a detached house. The heat loss from a terrace or semi-detached house would obviously be less, and the expenditure would depend on individual owners and their control of the temperatures, and the efficiency of the equipment, but the National Heating Consultancy state that the relativity between the fuel consumptions would remain constant.

SOLID FUEL FIRES

Stoves

Open fires burning wood, coal or smokeless fuel, or closed stoves consuming the same, provide that nostalgic kind of heat ('keep the home fires burning') round which the family gathers as the shadows flicker on the wall. Not so long ago central heating was considered a luxury, rather than taken for granted, and open fires were the only source of heat. Many fireplaces have been blocked up, as a matter of course, in conversion work to provide (with the surround and mantel removed) more wall space for furniture arrangements, positioning baths and general flexibility of space. Although many fireplaces could be reinstated, others could not without high cost. Depending on the cost of fuel, availability and type, heating by means of stoves and open fires is very much a viable method for these days because of the low initial cost of the appliances and the fuel they burn with the added bonus of the aesthetic delight they can give. Other facts to consider are that the fuel must be stored somewhere, the fires cleaned out and generally attended, that the fire risk, although not high, is greater than boiler heated radiator or warm air systems, and that flues should be in reasonable order and periodically swept. In addition, if the fireplaces have been blocked up and chimney stacks capped off, the cost of reinstating these will have to be taken into consideration. In many cases, in blocking fire openings the hearths will also have been removed and therefore some form of fire-proof hearth must be reinstated. Normally existing fire openings will be capable of accepting a slow burning stove or grate of some kind, although the choice may be narrow.

Solid fuel stoves with radiators

Many of the enclosed stoves, such as those by Rayburn or Parkray, are capable of heating a number of radiators up to about eight (150 ft², 13.94 m², of radiating surface) as well as hot water in a hot water cylinder. In summer neither the stove nor the radiators would be wanted and hot water would have to be heated by some other means such as an immersion heater.

AGA cookers (Glynwed Foundries Ltd.) are designed to produce a range for burning either solid fuel, gas or oil which, as well as being cookers, can produce heat for a 115–200 litres hot water cylinder. They produce enough heat at source to heat the kitchen itself.

Some solid fuel stoves have back boilers, i.e. hot water tanks incorporated into the back of the stove to produce a supply of hot water without a separate cylinder. Others (Redfyre) have stoves with extension ducts for supplying some warm air to the next room or space.

Solid-fuel central-heating boilers

These have been steadily developed over the years by the Coal Board. Boilers with a degree of automation to them, and also with forced draught equipment are on the market and must be seriously considered. They require more attention than fully automatic gas or oil boilers which, in the past 'age of affluence' was considered a drawback. They are still messier than oil and gas boilers and require storage for the fuel, and the ash. But the economics of the conversion job will demand consideration of solid fuel boilers as a possible choice for heating, especially as thermostatic control is also possible through dampers and manipulation of the draught.

GAS FIRED EQUIPMENT

Gas fires

These are much more sophisticated objects than the old fires with their fragile mantles which always seemed to be tottering on the brink of collapse, held in only by wire clips; to dismantle them for cleaning invited catastrophe.

The new models, although tending to be over-designed, are much more efficient and incorporate convection channels, in most cases, to get as much heat out of the casing as possible. Automatic ignition is also available either by battery or from a local electric point.

The fire will have to be built into an existing fire opening, unless it is in a flueless room in which case balanced flue types are available so that fresh air can be drawn in and burnt gases expelled from the equipment safely. Fire openings are best blocked in with blocks or bricks with a small opening for the fire flue at the back. Asbestos panels can be used as long as sufficiently robust and sealed at the edges. Gas convector units (Drugasar by Robinson Willey Ltd.) can be fitted on outside walls because of the need for a balanced flue to the outside air.

Gas water heaters

The Baxi Bermuda is a fire for fitting in an existing fireplace and also has a back boiler.

But otherwise gas water heaters are old friends known generically by laymen under the name of 'Ascots' (as in the same way plastic laminates are called 'Formica'). Several firms make gas instantaneous water heaters. New World (Gas Heating) Ltd. produce the Ascots, and Main Gas Appliances Ltd. have their range of water heaters. These heaters can supply hot water at a single point or multi points. The latter type can therefore serve a bath, basin, sink or other points near to it, depending on circumstances.

Instantaneous water heaters can be used even where a central boiler is provided. They are useful for providing a hot water point some distance from the rest of the system where it might be necessary to run long hot and cold water pipe lengths to a distant point if an instantaneous heater is not used. They only require a cold water supply which is usually from the tank, but can be off the main, although the local water board should be consulted in the latter case and may make special conditions. A stop cock should be fitted at the heater. Multipoint heaters will require flues to the outside, integral with the fittings, and good permanent ventilation to the room of 20 sq in (130 cm^2).

Single point heaters usually have no flue of their own so it is even more important that good permanent ventilation is provided. As the heaters will be usually in a bathroom, where people often retire if feeling ill, this point about ventilation is important. There have been accidents.

There are also gas water heaters that have their own flue and are connected direct to a hot water storage tank of maximum capacity 270 litres. New World (Gas Heating) Ltd. also make this type under the Ascot label.

Gas boilers

There have been considerable developments in the variety of gas boilers available. As well as the type with a conventional flue pipe that can be taken up outside the building to terminate at a reasonable height and position, the same type can be connected direct into an existing flue. In addition, there are the balanced flue type floor standing units which must be on an outside wall but do not need a conventional flue. A development of these floor units is the new forced extract balanced flue units which are very small and compact, can be mounted on the wall at a high level, but must again be on an outside wall.

Where the gas boiler is to be connected into an old flue, the whole height of the chimney must be lined internally with a flue liner to prevent the gases from the boiler attacking the lining of the old flue and causing discoloration to decorations. There is considerable moisture in the gases given off. Flues are often lined with flexible stainless steel lining tube such as that called Kopex, made by Uni-tubes Ltd. Although the linings are naturally costly, the gas boiler type for connecting into a flue is cheaper than one of the same size with a balanced flue. Conventional boilers need a vertical flue but do not need to be on an outside wall.

Balanced flue boilers must be on an outside wall. The flue device both takes in fresh air and expels exhaust gases. The siting of the flue must also relate to wind eddies and draughts externally.

Gas warm air

Warm air heating from a central gas boiler means air ducts run from the unit and terminating in outlet grilles in the rooms. There are variations on this basic idea. For instance, the unit can blow out warm air into the house, without ducting, which will give general heating but is not designed to maintain temperatures in distant rooms. It would be suitable for heating a large space. Fitting ducts and grilles into existing houses can cause considerable disruption because of the size of air ducts, both flow and return. But compared with the visual effect of radiators, and the disturbance involved in running pipes horizontally and vertically, warm air ducts and grilles may be well worthwhile. Warm air systems are also capable of a quicker response—a flick of a switch will have warm air flowing in the ducts almost instantaneously. The decision to use warm air may be a personal one: a preference for either radiant or air warmth may override practical considerations of installation.

Gas warm air units can also heat the hot water for the house if required. There are also warm air units similar to gas fired ones but fuelled with oil.

HEATING WITH OIL Oil-fired boilers can be enclosed in a casing and may look similar to gas units when at the smaller end of the domestic range. Boilers below about 20 kw are of the vapourising type; above they are usually the pressure-jet type. All oil fired boilers require conventional rather than balanced, flues and the pressure-jet units may make more noise than the vapourising type, or gas boilers. However oil boilers need oil tanks and a gravity feed oil line. There may be difficulty in placing the tank at a higher level than the boiler, due to site conditions. The tank will also need supporting on a base, probably brick, and a trench may be necessary for the oil line. It will have to be in a place accessible for the hose of the oil delivery tanker. It may be necessary to discuss this detail with a delivery company. It is possible in certain cases to pump the oil supply. If the oil tank is placed within the building, the room in which it is installed should provide a catchment pit sufficient to contain a full tank of oil should there be a leak in the tank itself. This might involve an upstand wall at the door threshold and an oil-proof floor and skirting material.

For the size of the oil tank, it is recommended that quotes should be obtained from the local supplier to assess the benefits of bulk delivery and provide a tank size to take advantage of this if money and site permit a large tank.

Obviously, the extra capital cost of an oil-fired installation must be weighed against a gas system where, perhaps, a gas service pipe has to be brought into the site. Oil fired boilers obviously have a strong claim in situations where there is no gas available. Oil can be used in some warm air units.

HEATING WITH ELECTRICITY The capital cost of installing electric heating is not as high as a radiator or warm air system using a central boiler. Individual heaters may already be in the client's possession and with the provision of extra socket outlets if necessary, the house can be warmed. However, the cost of heating with electricity is high on the normal day tariff, and if the house is heated with electricity, the water will probably also be heated in this way. This obviously requires no flue, oil tank, gas service pipe, flue, special ventilation, or take up any more space than a hot water cylinder requires.

To counteract the high daytime cost of electricity, there has for some time been the off-peak rate which has encouraged the development of heaters which will absorb electric heat at night and give it out during the day, either as heat or hot water. There used to be a boost period in the afternoon but this is not possible for new installations now. The types of off-peak electrical types are as follows.

Block storage heaters ('night storage' heaters)

These common heaters have a core of heat storage material and are very heavy. They give out heat during the day after storing it at night. If fitted with a fan, the output of heat is more controlled. Fan-assisted heaters can also be connected to an air duct system to blow air into several spaces. The size of the heaters and their number can be calculated to provide a correct, or desired, level of heat. Local electricity boards will make recommendations. The bulkiness of storage heaters can be a drawback.

'Electricaire'

Under this general heading come a range of large storage units for placing centrally in a building. The storage unit is highly insulated, and the heat given off by the core is circulated by a fan through air ducts to the whole house. Some models have a booster device to step up the heat output over a short period of, say, 20 minutes.

Underfloor heating

Electric cables can be laid in the concrete or screed of a floor and give off heat during the day in the same way as storage heaters, except that there can be no fan assistance. However, the cables are, of course, invisible and give a very pleasant overall warmth when buried in a ground floor under tiles, brick or stone paving. It is perhaps best used as background heat to some other heating, taking the chill off the concrete floor finish, but not raising the floor temperature too high as this can have an adverse effect on the feet of the occupiers. The ground floor slab should be insulated against loss of heat downwards and sideways. Sketches for thermal insulation are given in page 85. The cost of installing the cables (which can be withdrawable) makes underfloor warming an attractive proposition in new concrete slabs.

Electric ceiling heating

Apart from radiant and convector fires, oil filled radiators, infra-red heaters, fan heaters, tubular heaters and other electric heaters working off the usual day rate, there is electric ceiling heating.

Several firms have systems of electric heating panels. These come in pre-wired sheets and can be buried behind plaster or hidden behind suspended panel ceilings. They are mineral insulated and can be combined with insulation quilts. They are not run off the night rate, there being little storage capacity in the ceiling material, but can give instant response and can be thermostatically controlled.

White meter

Where off-peak electric power is consumed, the whole installation including lights and power can be used at a special rate if a 'white meter' is installed. Thus when low rates come into force between 11 p.m. and 7 a.m. (in most cases) all electrical equipment used after 11 p.m. or before 7 a.m. will be recorded at the 'white' meter tariff. This will also mean that off-peak equipment does not have to be wired back to a separate meter and time clock. A 'white' meter records for both normal and low rate consumption on separate dials within the meter, switching from one to the other on its own time clock.

OTHER FUELS FOR HEATING

Paraffin stoves

Have been used as a cheap form of heating for many years. They give off a smell, which can be nostalgic, but not to everyone's taste, and also a quantity of moisture which causes condensation difficulties unless ventilation is provided. They can be safe if sensibly positioned away from draughts and areas where they can be knocked over.

Bottled gas

Such as Calor gas, has been used for many years for cooking, lighting and heating. Some people prefer cooking on gas from whatever source. Gas cylinders are kept, preferably, out of the building and changed over regularly by the suppliers. They are connected by a small gas pipe to the various items of equipment.

OTHER SOURCES OF ENERGY

Solar heating

Heat from the sun may be made a more practical proposition in the '70s. With energy now so expensive, other sources may become competitive if not essential. Solar heat is a distinct proposition although unlikely to provide all the heat or hot water required. In converting a house, solar heating equipment might replace one side of a pitched roof. One basic idea is that the sun's rays, even on an overcast day heat water trickling through pipes down a slope under glass. This water can be re-circulated by pump to the top of the apparatus to be re-heated and can eventually enter the water service system to complement the heating or hot water supply for the house. Perhaps a more likely development will be the possibility of a patent piece of apparatus being devised which can be bought and set up on a roof or in a garden and 'plugged' into the house. Time will tell.

Wind power

There are several types of windmill (conventional horizontal axis, vertical cylinder, vertical axis which may be capable of being adapted for use in producing energy for house services. When the wind blows, electrical energy will be produced through a turbine. It would be an advantage to store this in batteries for use when the wind is not blowing. Alternatively it may become possible for the windmill to store energy in the form of compressed air, or to provide energy for a 'heat pump'.

Digester unit

Sewage and waste can be digested to produce methane gas and heat through anaerobic change and ways are being devised to use the energy released.

13 Insulation: Thermal and Sound

THERMAL INSULATION With the rapid increase in the cost of heating buildings, whichever fuel is used, the use of insulation in buildings is undergoing constant revaluation. Paradoxically, the increase in fuel cost is having an effect on the cost of making insulation material itself and it is not easy at the time of writing to predict whether this will tend to rule out some insulation materials which use oil based materials, as well as requiring a lot of energy to convert them to a suitable material with insulating characteristics.

The placing of insulation, and the choice of materials, for new buildings should be studied with a view to their use in any new structure added to an existing building either at ground or roof level. In Appendix 3, various insulating materials are shown compared by figures for thermal conductivity and resistivity to help in the selection of material.

There are various common sense factors to be considered. For instance, however much insulation is used, draughts from badly fitting doors and windows will cause discomfort and heat loss. Such basic faults as these should be corrected either by refitting the items, replacing them where defective as well as fitting draught excluding strips and sill units. It is hardly worth double glazing a window if heat can escape round the edges of the frame.

The Department of the Environment has issued figures showing the heat loss from various parts of a building, based on a between-the-wars semi-detached house. It is considered that about 35% escapes through the walls, 25% through the roof, 10% through the windows, 15% through various draughts and the remaining 15% goes into the ground.

Ideally all these parts should be insulated in some way.

Insulating the roof

The insulation of pitched roofs is comparatively simple. If an attic is not used except for the cold water tanks, expansion tanks and dead storage, it is probably best to lay the insulation over the ceiling joists. This will keep to a minimum the volume of the building to be kept insulated, but tanks and pipes above the insulation will themselves need insulation against frost damage. The usual method is to drape fibreglass quilt over the ceiling joists. The quilt should be a minimum thickness of 50 mm. However, an increased thickness would be better. Uncovered fibreglass in an attic can get covered in dust, perhaps blown in under the eaves, and can loose some of its insulating properties unless protected. This can be done by using a paper faced quilt as the top layer, or covering the whole laid quilt in polythene.

Alternatively, the quilt can be laid in strips between the ceiling joists, but this method is liable to leave gaps against the joists and may add to the labour costs by taking longer to lay.

Instead of fibreglass, one of the sheet insulating materials such as expanded polystyrene or urethane can be laid over or between the joists. Sheets can easily be cut to fit round obstructions but the ceiling hatch may have to be enlarged to get reasonable sized sheets into the attic space.

Roofs can also be insulated by pouring loosefill expanded vermiculite in between the joists to a thickness of at least 50 mm, but preferably more. Care should be taken to see that this light fill does not blow about through draughts in the attic space. It might be best to cover it with building paper or polythene to keep it clean and in position.

By placing roof insulation over or between the ceiling joists, the natural fresh air ventilation to the roof structure can be maintained. If for any reason the insulation has to be placed under the pitched rafters, fresh air to the roof space should be discouraged by sealing air passages at the eaves or perimeter, but ventilation must still be arranged to ventilate the rafters themselves if they are sealed under the roof finish of tiles, slates, etc.

If considerable reconstruction is taking place, and ceilings to the top floor are to be replaced, foil backed plasterboard may be used to increase the insulation regardless of what is used in the way of a 'blanket' in the roof space above.

In cases where the roof space has been converted to habitable space, insulation will have to be incorporated under the roof slope, or within the roof structure. Insulation material can be pinned under the rafters, perhaps using sheet materials as the ceiling finish. Alternatively, a blanket material can be packed between the rafters. If the blanket is hung under the rafters, difficulty may be found in fitting the ceiling finish over it. For instance, laying a match-boarded ceiling over fibreglass mat is not easy, as the tongues and grooves in the timber get jammed with loose material.

Alternatively, strips of rigid insulation can be cut to fit between the rafters so that the ceiling finish can be fixed firmly to the underside of the rafters. If plasterboard is used, foil backed should be used to add to the insulation.

Insulating an existing flat roof will require the destruction of either the roof finish or ceiling below. With a joisted roof, and a top finish in good condition, blanket or rigid insulation can be introduced between or underneath the rafters, with, in addition, perhaps a foil backed plasterboard fitted back under the structure.

In the case of a concrete slab roof, a layer of insulation can be added below, either fixed direct to the slab or suspended below it if the room height allows. Alternatively, insulation can be added on the top by the removal of the finish and application of insulation material below a new finish. This could be in the form of lightweight insulating screed or rigid insulation under a screed.

Insulating the walls

1 Solid walls in existing buildings can have their insulating characteristics improved by either lining the interior with insulation material or adding it externally, with a new weatherproof exterior finish

Depending on circumstances, the inner face of the wall could be insulated by:

a constructing an inner insulating block wall with cavity against existing wall

b battening the wall, fitting sheet or blanket insulation between the battens, and finishing with foil backed plasterboard or sheet wall finishing material

c using an insulating plaster inner wall lining, possibly combined with a corrugated damp proofing material such as 'Newtonite' where the air trapped in the corrugations would also have some insulating effect

2 Cavity walls. In spite of cavity walls having a likely superiority over solid in the matter of insulation, especially if the inner skin is made with insulating blockwork, the insulation can be increased not only by the methods noted above for solid walls, but also by filling the cavity by injection with urea formaldehyde foam. This system provides a 2 in (50 mm) foam-filled layer between the two leaves, but there has been considerable discussion on this type of insulation. Being injected into an unseen space, one cannot be certain that the whole cavity has been filled. Some private owners have been 'taken for a ride' and, on complaining of no saving on fuel bills, it has been discovered that little foam has been injected. Reputable firms, however, have methods of testing that the foam is spreading out in the cavity. Unsealed cavities such as at the eaves, below the DPC, or even into another property cannot always be detected and the foam may be being pumped into an unexpected area. Some injection firms pump in an amount of foam calculated to fill the cavity as far as can be ascertained on inspection.

In addition, there are worries about the effect of foam insulation on the cavity wall ties and whether, after a period of years, faults in the external brick might allow moisture to penetrate through the foam to the inner skin. However, the principle of foam filling cavities for increased insulation seems a good one, as it is comparatively inexpensive and leaves the building unaltered internally and externally.

The Cavity Foam Insulation Association can recommend reputable companies and carries insurance on the guarantee that the company should provide for the owner.

The cavities in walls can also be insulated with granulated mineral wool, such as Rentokil Ltd. 'Rockwool'. This is a loose dry material which is blown into the cavity through 50 mm holes drilled in the outside wall leaf, and it is claimed will not lead to a moisture 'bridge' across the cavity. The worry with this material is that it could settle in the cavity over the years. Ideally both foam and mineral wool may reduce wall heat loss by about 70%, a saving of perhaps 25% a year in fuel bills.

Insulating the Floor

Possibly 15% of a house heat loss may go down through the floor.

If the floor is a suspended timber floor, it is comparatively simple to lift floorboards, fit rigid or quilt insulation material between or over the floor joists and replace the boarding. If the insulation material is rigid and placed over the joists, the finished floor level will be higher than before which may involve changes to skirtings, doors, thresholds and staircases, depending on circumstances.

An existing concrete floor is more difficult to insulate without considerable expense. However, rigid insulation can be laid on the slab and screeded which will raise the floor level by some 40 mm (if previously screeded) or 75 mm if not. Alternatively, if a timber floor finish (strip) is laid on battens on an existing concrete slab, the space between the battens can be insulated with sheet or quilt. This method will again give a finished floor level some 60 mm above the slab top.

Where electric underfloor heating is to be installed, various suggested positions of insulation are shown in the sketch details. However, any ground floor should be insulated if at all possible and even carpet will help in this.

Insulating windows

Insulating windows with double glazing should reduce the 10% heat loss through windows. This has been a popular form of insulation but it is, on an average, a small source of heat loss in a typical building. However, its highest benefit is in increased comfort, as the cold feeling of single glazing can be disturbing.

If the glass panes are of a large size in the existing window, and the rebates are suitable, double glazed sealed units can replace them. Alternatively, an inner skin of glazing can be fitted using one of the patent systems. These are fixed across the whole window and frame and can sometimes be removed in the summer and stored elsewhere. Where the existing window is divided into many panes, or is a lattice window, it is either necessary to replace it or fit an inner window, to gain additional insulation.

However, as noted before, there is little point in spending money on double glazing if the casement itself does not fit tight, but allows draughts. There are various draught stripping materials, temporary and more permanent, that should be fitted to draughty windows before any double glazing is fitted, apart from the alteration and rehanging of the frames themselves.

Insulating doors, etc.

There is a 15% heat loss through draughts of all kinds, including badly fitting windows as discussed above.

Doors should also be checked over for draughts and excluders can be fitted. In addition, the gap at the bottom of most external doors should be draught proofed with a sill fitting such as those made by Duraflex Ltd.

Unused flues provide more than adequate permanent ventilation and should be reduced by register plates or similar, as long as some ventilation is still allowed to the flue. Unused or oversized ventilators and air bricks should be checked over and blocked if necessary, and if permitted in Building Regulations.

Curtains, Shutters, etc.

With the high costs of heating being all too apparent, consideration should be given to using special insulating or reflecting linings to curtains; or to hanging winter curtains in front or behind the summer ones to increase the 'blanket' quality of trapped air. It may become desirable to fit sheets of rigid insulation across windows behind curtains or blinds. They could be stacked elsewhere during the day, or even left in position in cold weather. The quality of light that percolates through rigid foamed polystyrene is not unpleasant.

Many houses have shutters and, if they fit well, these will help to keep the warmth in. As they usually fold tightly on themselves, it would not be easy to add insulating material to shutters. The next few years should see developments in ideas for increasing the insulation quality of curtains and shutters.

Insulation of a hot-water installation

Tanks full of expensive hot water should be insulated to a higher standard than hitherto. Loose fitting hot water cylinder jackets could be improved. In the absence of better designs, tanks could be enclosed in purpose-made casings filled with rigid or loose insulating material. But care must be taken to maintain access to immersion heaters and cylinder thermostats. There are some cylinder jackets made in rigid polystyrene. Hot water pipes can be lagged in rigid insulation material but this decision should be discussed with the heating engineer in case it conflicts with his design intentions.

SOUND INSULATION When a house is divided to form separate flats, the sound insulation between them becomes a factor in the success of the project. Sound transmission from one space to another is of two kinds: impact sound (e.g. stamping feet) and airborne sound (e.g. singing). However, sound insulation will probably have to cope with both kinds.

Impact Sound

To reduce the impact sound travelling from one space to another, the aim should be to prevent the transmission of the impact to the structure. The simplest way is to use a soft finish to the floor, i.e. carpet, sheet floor on sponge rubber underlay, or cork tiles over 8 mm thick. However, alternatively, or in addition, the floor can be altered to provide a 'floating floor'. This is a floor where the top surface is fixed to screed or battens which is then separated from the main structure by a quilt or isolating material. (See sketch details.) Success depends on there being no rigid connection between raft and structure, such as the screed leaking through the isolating material to form a rigid connection. Also the isolating layer must have, and be capable of keeping, sufficient resilience during the life of the building. Glass wool, mineral wool and expanded polystyrene are suitable although special forms are made for this purpose.

Airborne Sound

For practical purposes airborne sound insulation of a construction is controlled by four factors; mass, discontinuity, stiffness and uniformity.

Mass

Insulation increases about 5 dB for each **a** doubling of weight, **b** doubling of frequency per octave.

As the partition weight has to double to gain a further 5 dB insulation, there is a point where this becomes uneconomic unless a specially high sound reduction is needed. Flanking transmission of sound through side walls may be at a level where there is no point in increasing the weight of the

A New flooring on small
battens resting on a
sound-resisting blanket
draped over the existing
joists. Pugging such as
50 mm sand has been laid
over the ceiling below, but
care must be taken that an
existing plaster ceiling can
take the pugging load. A
new and stronger ceiling
construction would
probably be necessary
B The battens can
alternatively run between
the joists, to keep the new
floor level low
C A screed can be laid
over an absorbent blanket
in concrete floor con-
struction
D Also in concrete floor
construction, a timber
floating floor on battens
and sound-absorbent
blanket can be used
E Sound absorption can be
obtained by adding battens,
blanket and plaster to the
underside of a floor

Sound reduction details:
partitions plans
F A standard stud parti-
tion can be improved by
applying 25 mm wood wool
slabs to the studs before
plastering
G By staggering the studs,
sound transmission can be
reduced, but a wider partition will result. By adding
a blanket between the
studs, further reduction
can be obtained
H An existing partition
could be improved by
adding battens and plaster
or other sheet material over
the existing plaster face
I Smaller studs could be
used with a sound insulating blanket pinned to one
set of studs

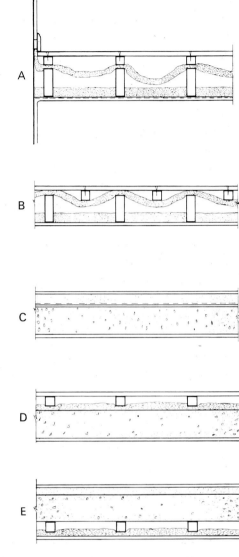

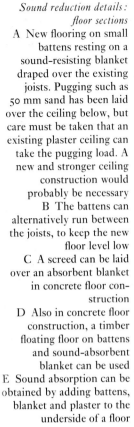

Walls

Floors

85

partition being constructed, beyond a certain point.

Discontinuity	Cavity walls and floating floors can produce effective discontinuity, but other factors such as structural stability and cost may affect decisions. Important practical points about cavity walls built for sound reduction are:

1 Wall ties should be avoided if possible, but if used, should be wire ties rather than rigid ones

2 The minimum useful width of cavity is 50 mm. Wider cavities greatly improve low frequency insulation

3 At the edges, where connection is inevitable, it is better to bond both leaves to the structure than attempt dissociation

4 Insulation is improved by sound absorption material in the cavity. This effect can be gained by using absorbent material for the two leaves, plastered on their room faces (woodwool slab, clinker block) or by the inclusion of a blanket of absorbent material in the cavity

Stiffness	In general 'flabby' materials are favourable to sound insulation. Where thin rigid materials are used (glass, plywood etc.) the wall can act as a drum. If possible weight should be increased by adding sheet lead or similar, and reducing stiffness, e.g. by grooving the back of ply sheets.

Uniformity	The insulation of partition or floor will be little better than that at its weakest point. Obviously doors or windows are potential weak points and will certainly be less good than the wall they are in. Similarly, holes, cracks and air porous materials will reduct the effectiveness of a partition or floor. Woodwool slabs, which can be air porous have a reduction of 8 dB for 50 mm thickness when un-plastered. Plastering increases this to 35 dB when applied both sides (which also of course increases the weight)

Sound absorption

The use of sound absorption materials will only affect the acoustic quality of sound in the room and will not reduce the amount of sound that can percolate through floor or wall. In fact sound absorptive materials are unlikely to be effective in providing sound insulation to adjacent spaces.

14 Value Added Tax as Applied to Conversions and Extensions

There is always the possibility that this tax may be varied from time to time either in the amount, the percentage, charged or the scope of it in relation to building work. The rate has already been changed generally since it was introduced in April 1973 and increased dramatically on petrol.

Basically, alterations to buildings are not taxed but repairs and maintenance are. H.M. Customs and Excise notice 715 describes tax in relation to the 'Construction Industry: Alterations and Repairs & Maintenance' and should be consulted. Although the architect or surveyor is bound to be involved in advising the client over the tax question, 'it is the supplier (that is the builder, contractor, decorator, or self-employed craftsman, as the case may be) who is, in the first place, responsible for deciding the VAT liability of any particular piece of work that he carried out'. Customs and Excise officers will advise over any particular problems.

If it is borne in mind that works of repair and maintenance are taxable, and alterations and new work not taxable, the problems should become more simple. Obviously a new extension does not bear tax but, say, re-decoration does. Rewiring a premises is taxable but not additional power or light points provided. It is difficult however to decide what proportion of an electrical account is attributable to each phase of the work.

Work in replacing defective items, such as windows, comes under 'Repair and Maintenance' and is taxable even if the new window is to a higher standard than the one replaced.

The Notice No. 715 gives lists of some basic building operations which are or are not taxable and it is likely that a particular problem may be found elucidated in the notice.

The architect or surveyor will of course charge tax on his own fees if he is a person or firm registered with Customs and Excise. He must register if the value of his taxable outputs (including zero-rated outputs) is, or is likely to be, more than £5000 a year.

Appendix 1: Job Check List

First meeting with client	Meet at home? Meet at site? Get approximate accommodation schedule for what is desired by client Discuss above generally Keep to practicalities or discuss the architecture depending on personality concerned Discuss equipment, furniture, possessions which have to be integrated in scheme Freehold or leasehold? Tenancies? Landlord's address? Any existing drawings available? Drawn survey required? Keys Existing written survey of premises available? Charges for survey, and description of likely fees, method of charging for phases, etc. Whether grant will be sought; warn of delay, assess likely amount obtainable per unit formed Discuss VAT applicable
Immediate Action After Meeting	Write confirming points discussed Request letter of appointment, if only for preliminary investigation Check whether premises is scheduled as being of historic interest, or in a conservation area Should quantity surveyor be employed? Should structural engineer be employed? Should services engineer be employed? Consider town planning aspect, whether permission likely to be required Check with landlord any likely constraints Take site photographs, including details Organise measured survey of premises, or obtain drawing by others. See Appendix 2 Send survey drawing to client for his information Sketch designs for alterations Discuss generally with local planning department

Should any other consultants be employed?

Second Meeting with client	Produce sketch design or designs and discuss Gain approval for one scheme to be worked up Take note of comments Discuss estimate of costs in general Discuss programme Decide to apply for town planning approval and/or building regulations approval
Action after second meeting	Draw up decided scheme Check any survey dimensions necessary for design details where accuracy might affect whole design possibility Discuss 'means of escape' with local authority and submit drawings for approval Draw up and submit drawings and forms for town planning, building regulation, historic buildings section, landlords' approval, after discussing with these departments Meet public health inspector on site and submit drawings for drainage approval after clarifying points at meeting if possible Submit estimate of cost of work and programme to client as foreseeable at this stage Preservation of trees Apply for clearance for 'underground rooms' regulations

Action after submissions for approvals	Decide with client whether to do no further architectural work until town planning and other approvals are received, or proceed with specification, details, sub contracts etc. Advise over fee for abortive work should planning approval be refused
	Confirm in writing
	Submit sample materials as necessary
	Party wall awards for all separate party walls
	Detailed drawings
	Obtain quotes on:
	    electrical layout
	    central heating
	    kitchen units, standard or special
	    flooring by specialist subcontractors
	    Electricity Board work
	    Water Board work
	    Gas Board work
	    Calor gas installation
	    ironmongery supply
	    sanitary goods supply
	    kitchen equipment supply

special windows
special fireplace or surround
damp-proofing subcontractors
GPO telephone installation
garden landscaping
metalwork

Form of Contract	Discuss with client method of choosing builder i.e. tenders
	negotiation
	management fee
	time and materials
	direct labour
	Insurance
	Choice of builders to tender, or negotiate
	To obtain grant, does local authority need more than one estimate from builders or subcontractors?
	RIBA contract form 'Articles of Agreement' or yellow minor works contract form or special written agreement
	Stipulate return of specification from builder with estimate, each item to be priced in margin or in manner requested by grant authority
Grant Application	On receipt of builder's estimate to be accepted make grant application
	Probable documents for grant applications:
	grant forms
	set of drawings showing existing and proposed work
	priced specification
	subcontractors' estimates for damp-proofing, electrical work, central heating or other heating and hot water work, and other sub-contracts or supplies noted before
	a note of architect's and consultant's fees
	evidence of ownership, title deed, land registration number, name of solicitor
	town planning approval form and other approvals noted as likely to be necessary above
	Inform successful tenderer or agreed builder of grant application and approximate date when grant approval is expected and work could start on site. Possibility of start to prevent further deterioration
	Inform unsuccessful builders and subcontractors or suppliers
Work on Site	Agree rates for daywork
	Get contract signed by builder and client

Warn builder to send in notice to building inspector or district surveyor

Pass estimates to general contractor (builder) from subcontractors and suppliers for acceptance and clarification of requirements for builder's work in attendance, if not done pre-contract

Temporary lighting and power

Discuss sequence of operation, agree programme

Minutes—taken by architect or contractor?

Regular or random meetings on site?

Permission required from contractor to subcontract some parts of work

Arrange integration of GPO telephone wiring

Organise samples, provided by architect, builder, or subcontractors or suppliers

Check programme, inform client of any delay

Check materials, workmanship and dimensioned accuracy

No work to be done on site on instruction of client direct. Inform client this is so, and that all instructions to the builder must come through and from architect

Refer to specification to remind contractor of its existence, from time to time

Take progress photographs

Issue variation orders

Monitor extra costs, inform client periodically

Appendix 2:
Site Measured Survey Check List

CHECK LIST	*Equipment*	Tape, long
		Tape, short
		Metre stick
		Damp meter
		Level
		Camera
		Ladder
		Torch
	Access	Keys, house, flats, rooms
		Estate agent's approval to enter
		Appointment with owner if occupied
	Site plan	Boundaries in relation to house
		Note fences, hedges, walls (heights)
		Steps
		Changes of level
		Trees, type
		Outbuildings
		Adjoining buildings
	Externally	Manholes and gulleys
		F.A.I.
		Incoming services:
		GPO
		Gas
		Elec. cable
		Water stopcock
		R.W.P.s
		Heights of areas, obstructions
		Road levels
		Cesspools, septic tank
		Wells
		Soakaways
		Heights to windows, eaves, cornices, plinths
		Count brick courses for inaccessible parts
		Draw pipes on elevations
		Wall creepers

Internally	Running dimensions
	Separate dimensions
	Diagonals to fix 'squareness' of rooms
	Floor to ceiling heights
	Floor thickness
	Wall thicknesses
	Incoming services
	Meter positions
	Sanitary goods
	Drain and waste runs
	Vents and grilles
	Boiler, hot tanks, cold tanks
	Radiators or heaters
	Run of joists and boards, with widths
	Heights of sills, windows, lintels
	Stair risers and treads
	Skirtings
	Architraves and doors
	Floor finishes
	Fireplaces, open or blocked, hearths, mantels
	Cornices, variety in rooms, staircases
	Roof structure, ridge height, sizes of members
	Centres of rafters, ceiling joists
	Check angle of roof pitch
	Record electrical layout

Details	Measure special items if they are to be reproduced
	Check special and critical parts where extension is proposed
	Check equipment critical dimensions and service requirements
	Measure owner's equipment, furniture if to be incorporated

Appendix 3: Insulation: Relative Values

The figures are taken from *Thermal Insulation of Buildings* published by H.M.S.O. for the D.O.E. Reference to this book is recommended for amplification and explanation of the figures, as well as further information on the 'U' values of various composite constructions.

	Thermal conductivity w/m°c K	Thermal restivity m°c/w I K
Artificial aggregate loose fill	0.12–0.15	8.3–6.7
Expanded vermiculite loose fill	0.062	16.1
Asbestos fibre spray	0.037–0.058	21.4
Asbestos insulation board	0.11–0.14	9.3–7.1
Concrete: clinker aggregate	0.54–0.75	1.8–1.3
Concrete: expanded clay aggregate screed	0.19–0.34	5.3–2.9
Concrete: artificial lightweight aggregate screed	0.34–0.40	2.9–2.5
Concrete: expanded vermiculite roof screed	0.15	6.7
Concrete: foamed slag screed	0.29–0.45	3.4–2.2
Concrete: no fines	0.84–0.98	1.2–1.0
Corkboard	0.040	25.0
Fibre insulation board	0.053	18.9
Glass fibre mat	0.039	25.6
Glass fibre roof boards	0.033	30.3
Glass fibre rigid slabs	0.033	30.3
Lightweight plaster (vermiculite aggregate)	0.23	4.3
Mineral fibre, mat, quilt, faced	0.036	27.8
Mineral fibre, rigid slab	0.036	27.8
Mineral, slag or rock fibre (cavity wall filling)	0.045	22.2
Expanded polystyrene, sheet	0.035	28.6
Rigid urethane board	0.023	43.5
Urea formaldehyde foam (cavity wall filling)	0.030–0.036	33.3–27.8
Compressed straw slabs	0.098–0.11	10.2–9.1
Wood wool slabs	0.074–0.11	13.5–9.1

Examples

EXAMPLE 1
Coleshill, Berkshire
Architect: Kit Evans

On the fringe of the Cotswolds, this 'U' shaped building enclosing a paved courtyard was the stable and laundry block associated with a fine italianate country house unfortunately destroyed by fire. The owner obtained the use of one wing of the stone building which before conversion was one large high space with massive roof trusses overhead.

A deck was slung across the centre of the room to form a first floor level, and a further deck hung at truss level to one side of the first floor to provide a bed gallery. The kitchen was built in a sort of 'pulpit' also above the first floor, with a bathroom below it, again at a different, lower, level from the first floor deck. None of the floors thus cover the whole plan area: there are always voids giving views down to the stone ground floor.

View across the dining space to the high level kitchen 'pulpit', with sitting area on the left.

*Key to drawings. Not all
numbers shown below
will be found in every
example.*

0 Void
1 Living
2 Dining
3 Bedroom
4 Kitchen
5 Study
6 Bathroom
7 Store
8 Terrace
9 Gallery
10 Playroom
11 Laundry
12 Garage
13 Studio
14 Future extension or
area for renewal
15 Conservatory
✳ separate w.c.

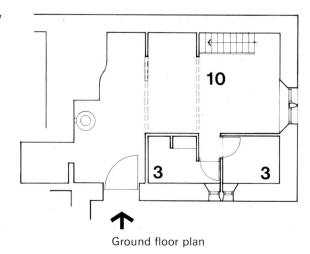

Ground floor plan

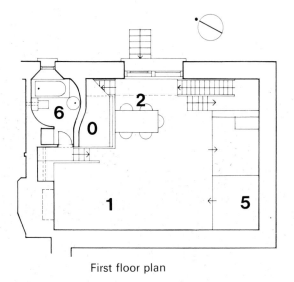

First floor plan

Second floor plan of kitchen

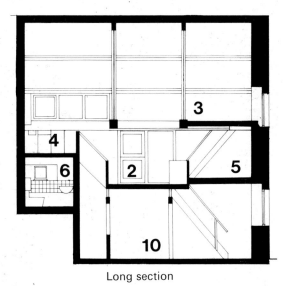

Long section

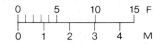

As time elapsed, rooms were required for two children which were built on the ground floor, a study was constructed at first floor level by building across one of the voids, and higher still, a further deck was hung off the roof truss for a model train layout area. At all times, however, the feeling of decks criss-crossing a large high barn-like space has been maintained which is the particular interest of this example. The opportunity for the addition of extra floor space when required for an expanding family was anticipated from the start by the general system of sturdy construction and forthright detailing that was developed and carried through into the additional work that has been done from time to time; part of a continuous process of extension and development within the original shell of this building.

Heating is provided by a large stove burning timber on the ground floor, an open fire at first floor level and individual electric heaters as required.

View from high level kitchen through old roof trusses to bedroom gallery.

The dining area, with
kitchen up short flight to
the left, with void to ground
floor below.

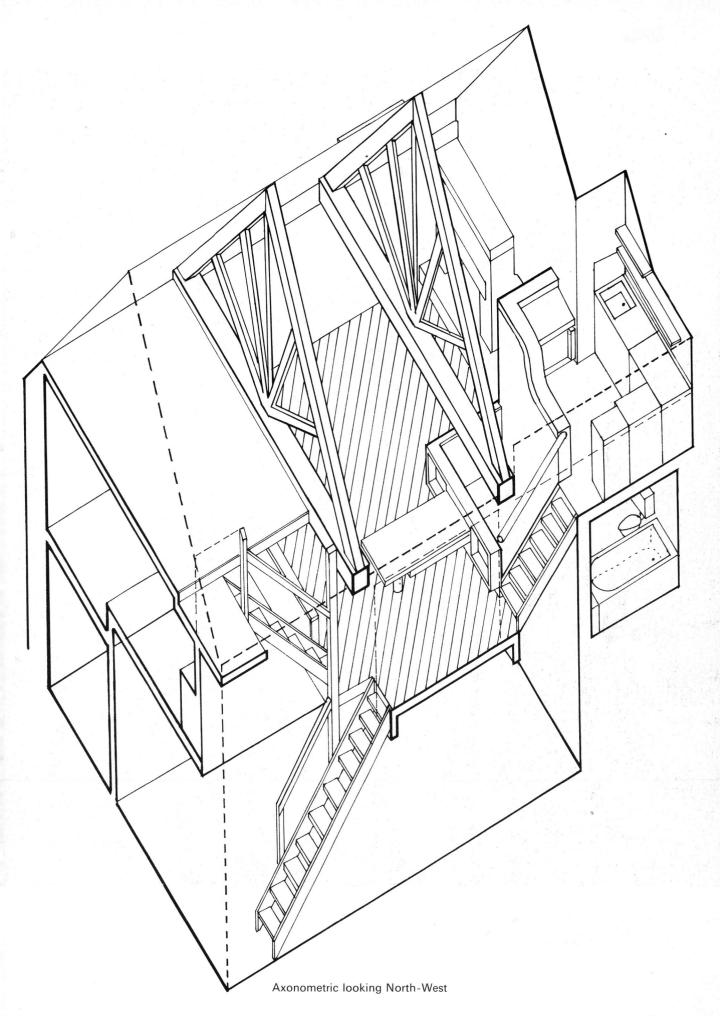

Axonometric looking North-West

99

EXAMPLE 2
**House in Islington,
London
Architect:
Michael Tilley**

A terrace house of about 1800, with basement, ground and first floors, has been extended at the ground floor half level across its full width. In addition, the whole interior of the house has been stripped down and cleared out to leave a very simple, even austere, atmosphere. This same feeling also extends in to the new part of the house so that the transition from Georgian proportions to something more 'Corbusian' is easily made. The fully glazed end to the room looks into a densely planted city garden. Building the garden extension almost completely across the house width has cut out daylight to the basement on that side. But by opening this part of the house up to the open stair arrangement and horizontally through to the kitchen, this fact is not very evident and the space feels like a natural extension to the

The new extension has fair-faced block work walls, a natural timber boarded ceiling and stained timber window and door, which leads to a small walled garden.

100

kitchen. In fact it is sometimes used as a dining area.

In remodelling the house, the windows were removed and single pane ones substituted. It is usual to replace windows to match the existing or original type. But where the proportions of the brick openings are made more evident by fitting single panes, the elevation takes on the look of one of those 18th-century steel engravings with dark windows. The proportions of brick to void read strongly. I feel this change of glazing design within an existing opening is a legitimate alteration. It is where the new inner skin of a building, that has been altered internally to suit the needs of the contemporary inhabitants, shows through to the outside. It is a clue that the interior has been changed.

The interior of the existing house has also been altered. The bathroom walls have been lined with pine boarding concealing the pipe work.

Key to drawings. Not all numbers shown below will be found in every example.

0 Void
1 Living
2 Dining
3 Bedroom
4 Kitchen
5 Study
6 Bathroom
7 Store
8 Terrace
9 Gallery
10 Playroom
11 Laundry
12 Garage
13 Studio
14 Future extension or area for renewal
15 Conservatory
* separate w.c.

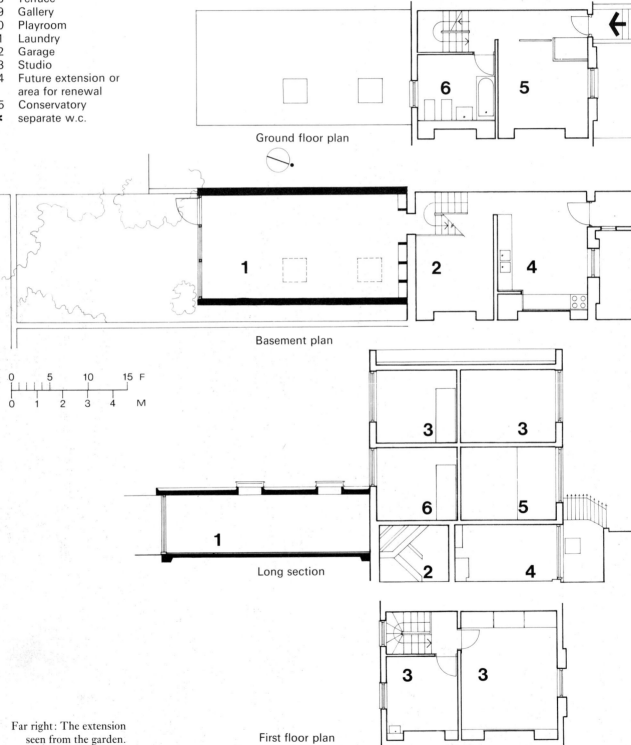

Ground floor plan

Basement plan

0 5 10 15 F
0 1 2 3 4 M

Long section

First floor plan

Far right: The extension seen from the garden.

**EXAMPLE 3
Converted farm
buildings, Swerford,
Oxfordshire
Architect:
Harry Teggin
and David Taylor**

The old farmhouse was in a bad state when bought for conversion into a house. It is perhaps not a conventional farm house.

Its smallish arched windows and three storeys make it untypical. But the architects have carried out alterations to maintain the sturdy feel of the stone building, to emphasise its solidity by cutting slots and doorways through the thick walls, opening up views along and across to reduce any feeling of constriction in a building which was only 12 ft (3.64 m) wide.

But the owners also wanted a large new room and additional bedrooms. These have been added in a new block at the end of the old farm house in line with its long axis. The walls are again Oxford stone but the living room, which has superb views over the rolling lush farmland, is a steel and glass affair totally, but successfully, different from the rest. The outline of the old walls of farm buildings that had to be cleared away have been kept to define the various outdoor spaces and to provide a framework for future landscaping. As I have discussed elsewhere, the construction of whole or part of an extension to an existing building in a totally different 'architecture'

The old farmhouse, itself reorganised, has been extended to the right with a flat topped stone linking structure cradling a brown glass living room at first floor level. The old stone walls run on to the barn at the right.

can enhance both the new and old and set off a reaction between them to their mutual advantage. Architectural history plays its part, of course. In this case one is reminded of the contrast in stone walling and plate glass as shown in Marcel Breuer's exhibition pavilion at Bristol done with F. R. S. Yorke during the former's short stay in England before the 1939–45 war. And again, Philip Johnson's Wiley house in Connecticut placed a glass pavilion living room on a rough stone ground storey to make the same strong contrast between man-made and earth-hewn materials.

There is often a problem in joining a new extension to an existing building. If the building to be extended is complete in itself and it is desired to maintain evidence of its original size and form, the extension can be connected by a 'flash-gap' structure across which the spark of a successful union can fly! In this case, there is a vertical glazed strip separating new and old; and also to get from the study to the steel and glass living room needs a journey across a short bridge at first floor level. Flash-gap links are also extremely useful for taking up, or making, changes of level.

The brown glass living room with terrace on the right and enclosed bedroom court on the left.

105

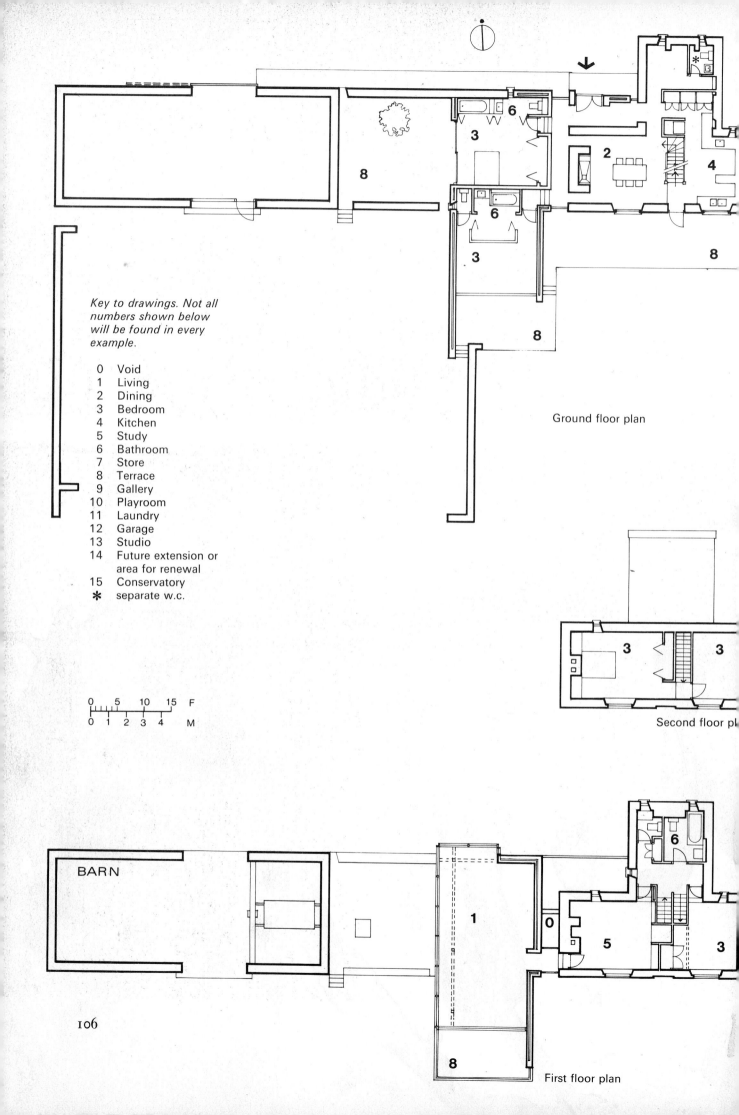

Key to drawings. Not all
numbers shown below
will be found in every
example.

0   Void
1   Living
2   Dining
3   Bedroom
4   Kitchen
5   Study
6   Bathroom
7   Store
8   Terrace
9   Gallery
10 Playroom
11 Laundry
12 Garage
13 Studio
14 Future extension or
    area for renewal
15 Conservatory
*   separate w.c.

Ground floor plan

Second floor plan

BARN

First floor plan

The interior of the living room which is entered from the left and has fine views over the Oxfordshire countryside.

Below: Looking through a doorway beyond the dining space on the left to the staircase and kitchen. The stair is painted dark blue, the kitchen yellow, the old stone walls white.

Below right: The entrance hall. The front door is at the end on the right.

**EXAMPLE 4
Kidlington,
Oxfordshire
Architect:
Martin Sylvester**

Although alterations have been made to several parts of this large house, the main part of the building operation was concerned with the living room extension.

The pitched roof of the main building has been extended down over the new living room but large plate glass windows have been introduced with complete success. The ceiling is high, the finish being under the rafter slope, with trusses exposed.

The large, rather grand, fireplace and chimney stack keep the scale of the room large but straightforward. The materials used are the popular ones for conversion work of the '60s and early '70s; natural timber boarding, brick paviors, natural brick, quarry tiles and plate glass. Will we be able to date this type of conversion architecture within a few years in the future?

The garden end of the new extension.

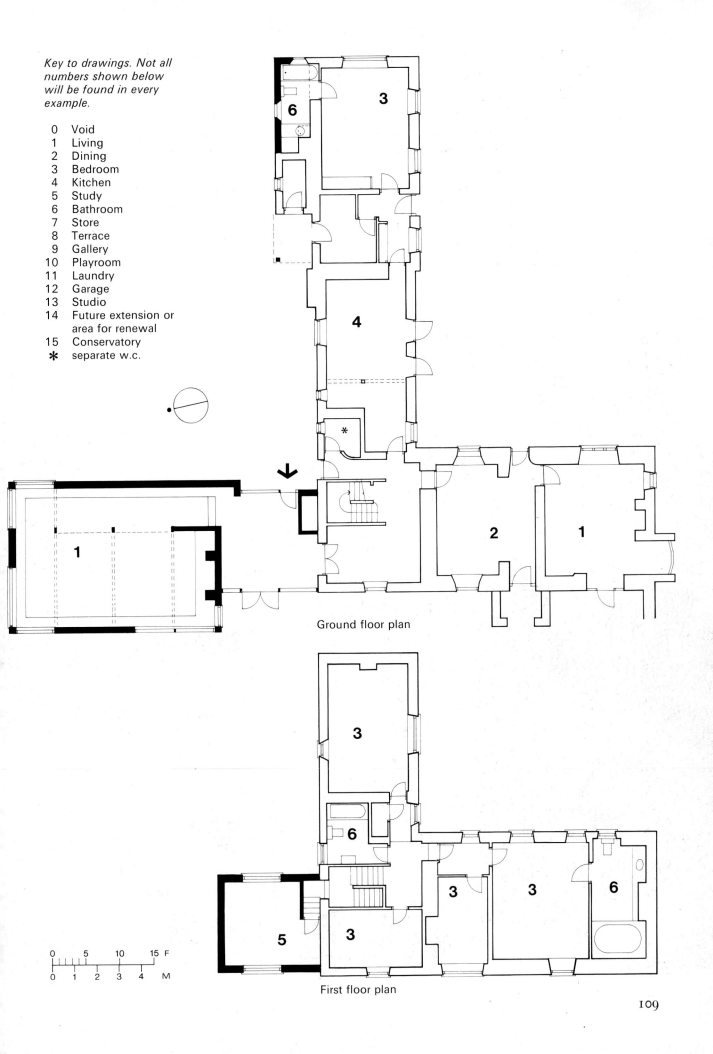

Key to drawings. Not all
numbers shown below
will be found in every
example.

0   Void
1   Living
2   Dining
3   Bedroom
4   Kitchen
5   Study
6   Bathroom
7   Store
8   Terrace
9   Gallery
10 Playroom
11 Laundry
12 Garage
13 Studio
14 Future extension or
    area for renewal
15 Conservatory
*   separate w.c.

Ground floor plan

First floor plan

0   5   10   15 F
0   1   2   3   4   M

Right: The side of the new room houses the books with a wide quarry tile shelf at low level.

Far right: The new entrance hall has a quarry tile floor. The entrance to the living room is on the right.

Below: The new room rises high into the roof space.

Below right: The new extension is built with stone walls and stone slates as the original house, but the windows are large and successfully different.

**EXAMPLE 5
House in Camden,
London
Architect:
John Winter**

The peculiarities of the site dictated the cranked plan for this extension. The architect has made a virtue of this restricted site boundary by 'fanning' the new extension façade round a pivot point, the lower level windows being on one radius, the upper on another. To prevent restriction inside, double heights have been introduced to liberate the space and to allow light to filter down into the interior. There is also a narrow gallery which leads like a bridge across to the wedge-shaped terrace at the upper level. This bridge is lit from the party wall side by a large area of side glazing from which light pours down to the kitchen area below. This is not a large extension but there is a lot 'going on' in three dimensions.

Key to drawings. Not all numbers shown below will be found in every example.

0 Void
1 Living
2 Dining
3 Bedroom
4 Kitchen
5 Study
6 Bathroom
7 Store
8 Terrace
9 Gallery
10 Playroom
11 Laundry
12 Garage
13 Studio
14 Future extension or area for renewal
15 Conservatory
✱ separate w.c.

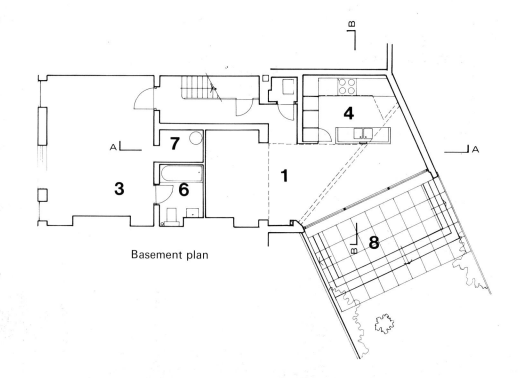

Basement plan

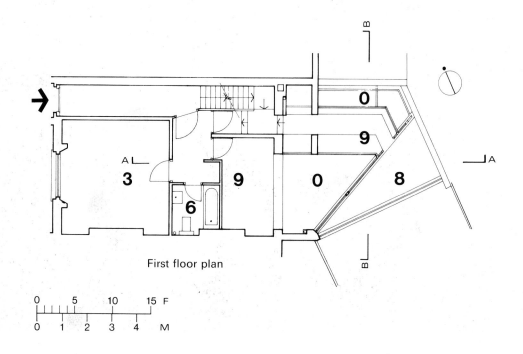

First floor plan

0   5   10   15 F
0 1 2 3 4 M

112

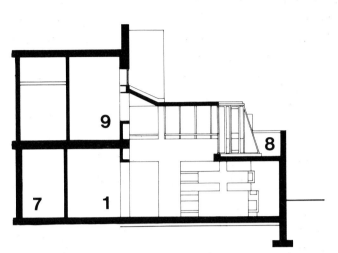

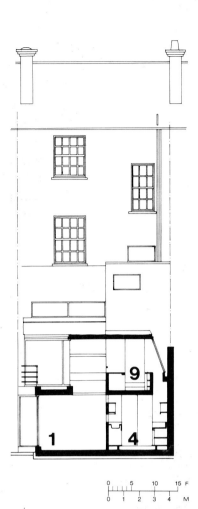

View from the living room towards the garden terrace running away at an angle to the right. On the left is the kitchen and above is the soffite of the triangular terrace.

Right: The internal gallery looks over the living room below to the terrace.

Below: The garden elevation. The glass at high level allows light to flood down to the living room making this view unusually transparent.

**EXAMPLE 6
Converted Farm
Buildings, Meon
Valley, Hants
Architect:
Adrian Gale**

With the reorganisation of so many farms, and with the trend towards amalgamation of small farms into larger ones, this sort of property is being released for other uses.

At first sight a long narrow range of farm buildings such as this might not seem a very suitable subject for conversion. But the architect has made a virtue of the restricted width of the buildings by not adopting a rigid corridor system with rooms off it, but by opening up spaces off the circulation route in an informal way. The existing buildings were wide enough at one end to make a reasonably large living room, and this part was substantially rebuilt to give large windows looking over the courtyard garden and across to the range of other redundant farm buildings which the owner hopes to make habitable in later phases of the work.

What is also interesting in this example is that the architect has eschewed any quaintness or 'folksyness' in his approach. Simplicity, even severity has been a principle in the detailing of the cupboards, kitchen, hearth and fireplace. A country farm is not necessarily the place to display the hand of great reverence for past forms and details which so often ends in sentimentality, or a genteel atmosphere. In fact the functional quality of so many farm buildings lends itself to the reflection of a similar quality in the detailing of the converted building.

The flint walled farm buildings have been re-fenestrated, and a living room formed at the end of the range.

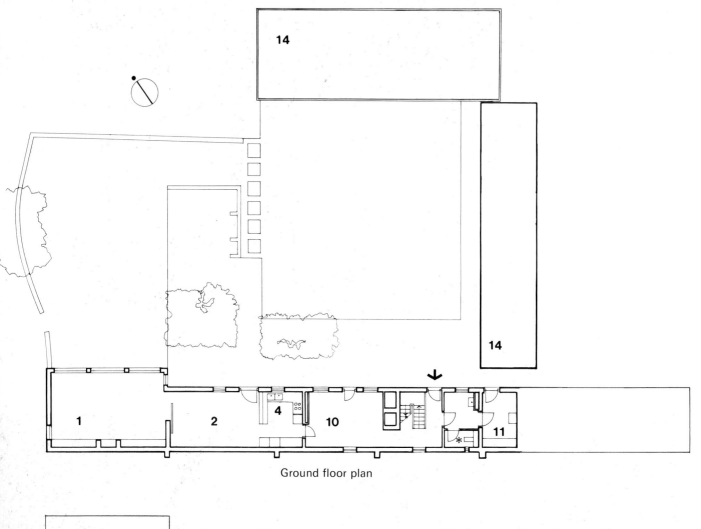

Ground floor plan

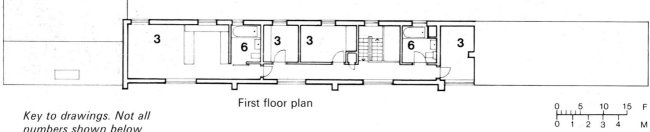

First floor plan

*Key to drawings. Not all
numbers shown below
will be found in every
example.*

0	Void
1	Living
2	Dining
3	Bedroom
4	Kitchen
5	Study
6	Bathroom
7	Store
8	Terrace
9	Gallery
10	Playroom
11	Laundry
12	Garage
13	Studio
14	Future extension or area for renewal
15	Conservatory
*	separate w.c.

Right: The pine french doors of the living room look out to the garden court, old barn and linking block which are to be converted in due course.

Below: Looking from the living room through to the dining room and kitchen. The opening can be closed by a large pine veneered sliding door.

**EXAMPLE 7
Lowther Village,
Cumberland
Architects:
Johnston & Wright**

Lowther Village was built to the designs of Robert Adam (although these were not necessarily for this specific site), and was constructed about 1770 but described as still incomplete in 1802. Sir James Lowther, who later became Earl of Lonsdale, was one of the most powerful and least popular provincial landowners of his time. He died universally hated in 1802, 'a madman too influential to be locked up' (Carlyle). Adam's design was one of the earliest of schemes incorporating crescents and squares, ideas which had excited Wood at Bath and later John Nash.

This ideal village was intended for workers on the estate and was also to incorporate a carpet factory. It was unsuccessful on both counts, was never completed or inhabited in full.

The present regeneration of such a significant complex has been carried out by the architects for the Lowther and District Housing Association with the aid of grants including one from the Historic Buildings Council. It has been mainly a case of reconstruction of the existing fabric, such as windows, chimney stacks and doors, fitting up the interiors and reconstructing and reorganising staircases.

The other courtyard group with two-storey buildings and single-storey linking blocks.

One of the courtyard
groups, with an old stone
pump in the foreground.

The quadrant buildings
from the entrance road.
They have a basement floor,
invisible in this view, which
looks out of the convex side.

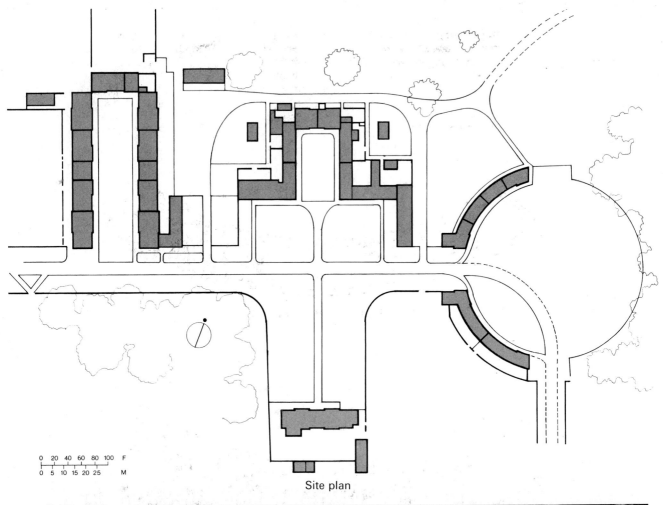

0 20 40 60 80 100 F
0 5 10 15 20 25 M

Site plan

The rear side of the
quadrant shows basement,
ground and first-floor levels,
the latter with roof lights.

122

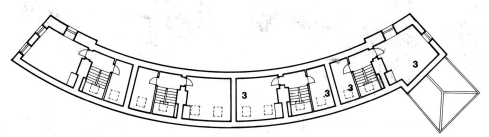

Key to drawings. Not all
numbers shown below
will be found in every
example.

0	Void	2	Dining	10	Playroom
1	Living	3	Bedroom	11	Laundry
		4	Kitchen	12	Garage
		5	Study	13	Studio
		6	Bathroom	14	Future extension or
		7	Store		area for renewal
		8	Terrace	15	Conservatory
		9	Gallery	*	separate w.c.

First floor plan, Quadrant

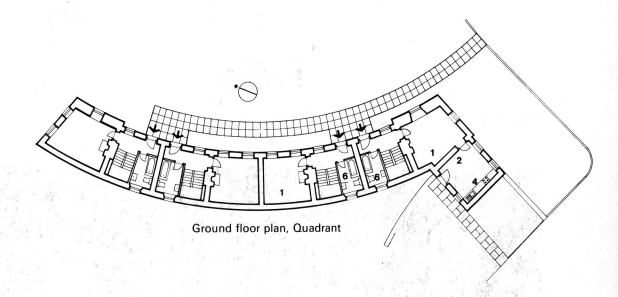

Ground floor plan, Quadrant

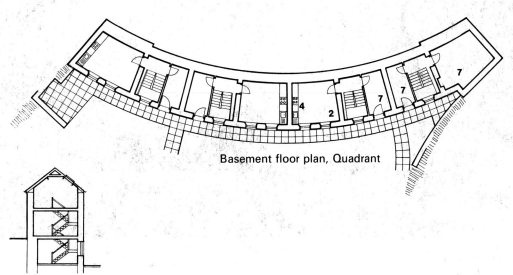

Basement floor plan, Quadrant

Cross Section through staircase, Quadrant

**EXAMPLE 8
Pimlico, London
Architect:
Stout and Litchfield**

In the dense Pimlico housing district, space is at a premium. In most cases the houses only have dark yards at the back and few gardens of any reasonable size. But there are the old coal vaults under the pavements which can sometimes be put to use as a bathroom or WC, although the cost of a guaranteed water proofing system may force reconsideration.

In this scheme the architects have come up with the brilliant idea of opening up these vaults into the 'areas' surrounding the corner house. They are usually bricked up with doors for access but by clearing the enclosing walls and doors away, the shape and depth of the vaults can be opened up to views from the interior of the house. With good artificial lighting and sensitive planting, this gives a feeling of space and openness to what is often a dark basement in this type of house.

The house has been thoroughly altered to provide two large flats with two floors each. The upper flat has got some outside terrace space for sitting out on. The architects are known for their personal style which tends to eschew the rectangular and embrace diagonal planning and irregularity. In this case, the fact of the building being a corner terrace one with light on two sides has suggested a breakaway from the original rectangular room layout. This has led to a thorough remodelling of the interior, and shaping of the basic structure to support the idea. One may not approve of such an approach to a house of this basic plan type, but it is done with such panache and sympathetic detailing that one is convinced.

Key to drawings. Not all numbers shown below will be found in every example.

0	Void
1	Living
2	Dining
3	Bedroom
4	Kitchen
5	Study
6	Bathroom
7	Store
8	Terrace
9	Gallery
10	Playroom
11	Laundry
12	Garage
13	Studio
14	Future extension or area for renewal
15	Conservatory
*	separate w.c.

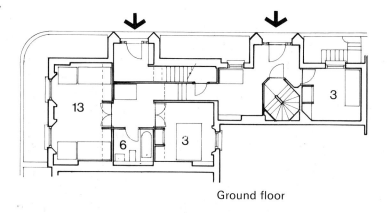

Ground floor

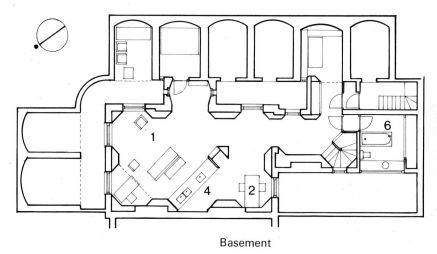

Basement

The elevation of the house showing the faceted entrances.

An upper floor room, showing main stair opened up to the space, and a curved plastered drum providing some privacy to the study beyond.

Far right: View from a vault under the basement, across the area, to a new basement window.

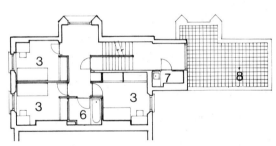

Third floor plan with mezzanine

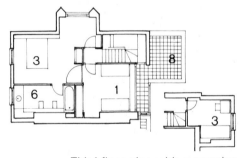

Second floor plan

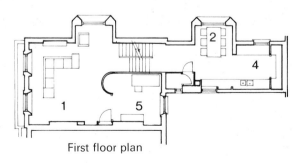

First floor plan

Above: Looking from the
kitchen across the basement
to the enlarged windows
showing the opened-up
coal vaults beyond.

**EXAMPLE 9
Chelsea, London
Architects:
Charlotte and Francis
Baden-Powell**

Although originally a small terrace house on three floors including basement, the architects have, over a period of 15 years or so, made considerable alterations to provide for an expanding family and living-in 'help'.

The first items to be tackled were the provision of a kitchen and bathroom in a rear extension set over to one side to allow light to the ground floor on the garden side.

Work to the new storey on the roof followed. So often an existing roof is found to have served its useful life and to be an embarrassment and a drain on maintenance funds, especially in London where there are so many central valley gutter roofs which are a common source of trouble. Where a roof needs considerable reconstruction, it is a good moment to consider providing a new one at a higher level so as to give extra space on top of the house.

The living room seen from the dining daïs with study area on the right.

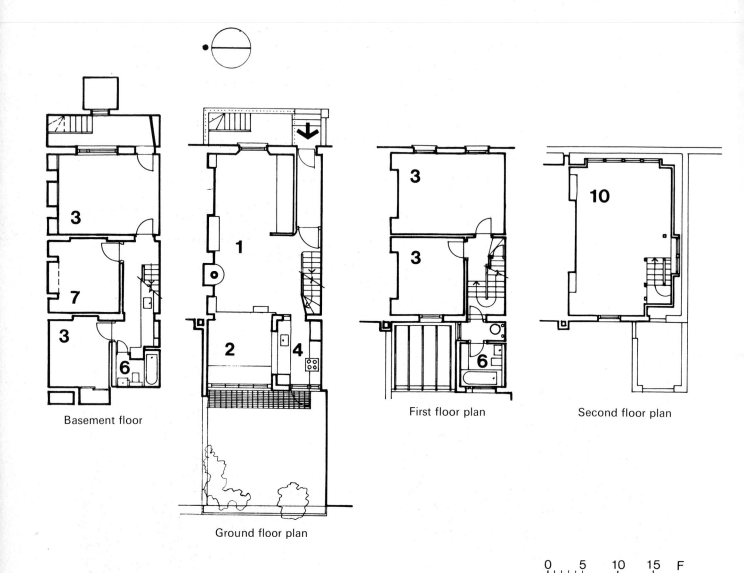

Basement floor

Ground floor plan

First floor plan

Second floor plan

0   5   10   15   F
|----|----|----|----|
0   1   2   3   4   M

Key to drawings. Not all
numbers shown below
will be found in every
example.

0   Void
1   Living
2   Dining
3   Bedroom
4   Kitchen
5   Study
6   Bathroom
7   Store
8   Terrace
9   Gallery
10   Playroom
11   Laundry
12   Garage
13   Studio
14   Future extension or
     area for renewal
15   Conservatory
*   separate w.c.

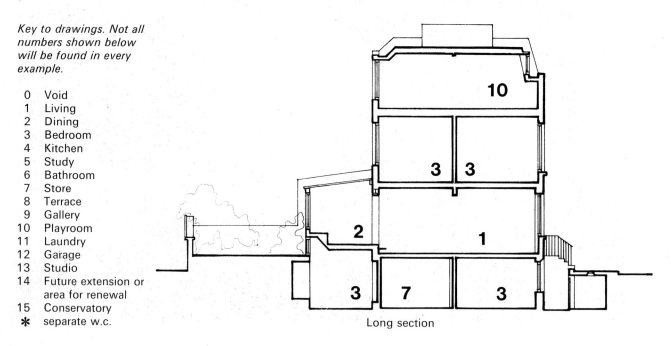

Long section

Having previously opened up the ground floor, the next alteration was to extend it towards the garden to give a dining space. The old kitchen side window became a hatch and so as to maintain as much light as possible in the centre of the house, the extension was fully glazed with sliding sashes, and patent glazed roof.

In order to provide adequate light to the basement garden room, the dining room extension was built at a higher level, as if on a dais. The steps up to it also form additional seating to the living area. The change of level, based on functional requirements ends up as aesthetically pleasing too.

The old kitchen side window has been altered to provide a hatch into the new dining space.

Above: The raised floor of
the dining space shows
where the extension was
built and the old external
wall removed. The change
of level is not only pleasing
in itself but allows a window
to the basement room
below.

Right: The garden side of
the house.

EXAMPLE 10
Notting Hill, London
Architects:
Anthony and Wadley

The original building had rooflights to provide a studio. The architects have carried out a drastic revision to the interior of an otherwise not very distinguished building. By adding a sleeping 'deck' slung from the existing roof, which has been carefully reorganised and cleaned up, the whole scheme has been given a special structure of interlocking timbers which dominates the space and makes it seem larger than it really is. The tubular steel stair structure merges neatly into a vertical ladder to the sleeping deck hatch. At present the building has been altered only from the first floor upwards; the ground floor is still garage and storage space. However, there is more than enough of that, so there are proposals to carry out a further stage of alteration to provide a small flat at the rear of the ground floor.

This is therefore one of those conversions where there is little to tell one from the outside that the interior has been drastically remodelled. Having retained the old studio rooflights and slung the 'deck' up at plate level, light filters through the expressed timber structure down to the main first floor, which is also lit from front and back.

Looking from the sitting area to the kitchen and showing the triangulated gallery framing lit by the existing roof lights.

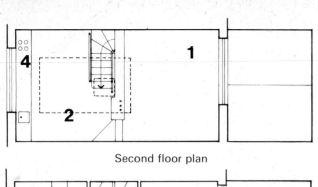

Second floor plan

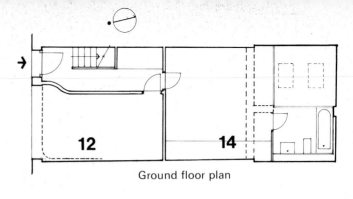

Ground floor plan

First floor plan

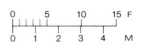

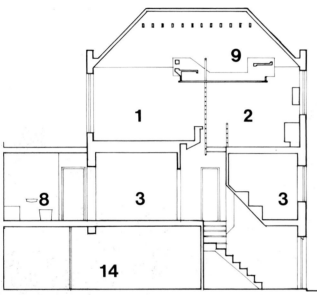

Long section

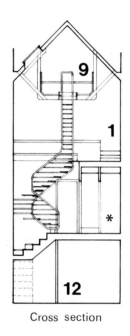

Cross section

Key to drawings. Not all
numbers shown below
will be found in every
example.

0   Void
1   Living
2   Dining
3   Bedroom
4   Kitchen
5   Study
6   Bathroom
7   Store
8   Terrace
9   Gallery
10 Playroom
11 Laundry
12 Garage
13 Studio
14 Future extension or
     area for renewal
15 Conservatory
✱   separate w.c.

Far right: The tubular
handrails change effortlessly
into a ladder to the
suspended gallery above.

Right: The suspended
gallery with the top of the
access ladder. The carpet
obscures the floor trap door.

134

EXAMPLE 11
Mews House,
Kensington, London
Architect:
Peter Collymore

The mews house before conversion had garage space for 3 cars (or horses) on the ground floor and various small rooms upstairs originally for housing the grooms and carriage drivers. The owner only required space for one car, but wanted to open up the cluster of rooms on the first floor to give one large space. By the use of a spiral staircase, the maximum space was liberated on the ground floor to give three bedrooms and an internal bathroom, and at the same time ensuring that one arrived near the centre of the open first floor. The sculptural beauty of spiral stairs can make its full impact in this situation. The stair is enclosed in a stud and plaster drum which is taken up to form a curved white plaster parapet on the first floor. This stair is a special one constructed of multi-plywood for treads and risers and put in compression by use of a steel tension rod at the centre to a design by Neave Brown RIBA. Double glazed 'Carda' windows were used to reduce noise from a railway which runs close to the back of the house.

The kitchen is placed at the eastern end of the first floor in an open arrangement which also includes the gas central heating boiler. The whole first floor is finished with maple strip flooring, the ground floor a mixture of cork, carpet, and vinyl tiles in the bathroom.

The first floor with spiral staircase arriving in the centre of the space. Before conversion, this level was divided into four small rooms.

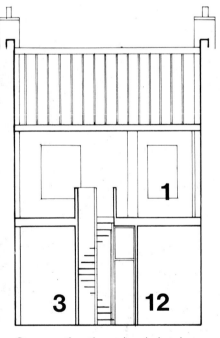

Cross section through spiral staircase

Key to drawings. Not all numbers shown below will be found in every example.

0 Void
1 Living
2 Dining
3 Bedroom
4 Kitchen
5 Study
6 Bathroom
7 Store
8 Terrace
9 Gallery
10 Playroom
11 Laundry
12 Garage
13 Studio
14 Future extension or area for renewal
15 Conservatory separate w.c.

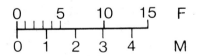

The specially designed
multiply timber staircase,
set in a plastered studwork
'drum', spirals up to the
open plan first floor.

The dining table and open
kitchen occupy one end of
the first floor.

*Key to drawings. Not all
numbers shown below
will be found in every
example.*

0   Void
1   Living
2   Dining
3   Bedroom
4   Kitchen
5   Study
6   Bathroom
7   Store
8   Terrace
9   Gallery
10 Playroom
11 Laundry
12 Garage
13 Studio
14 Future extension or
      area for renewal
15 Conservatory
✳   separate w.c.

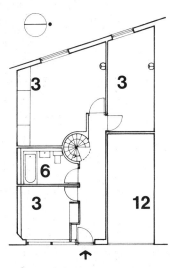

Ground floor plan

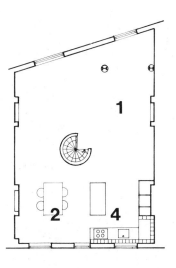

First floor plan

The front of the mews house. The original ground floor was totally given over to garages. The old windows were replaced with single-pane double-glazed pivot windows.

EXAMPLE 12
Barn Conversion,
Mapledurwell
Architect:
Jacob Blacker

A group of farm buildings has been converted into three separate dwellings. The natural court plan, with one open side, lent itself to division into three units. Only one of these, the spiral stair house, is shown in detail here. The existing timber frame and trusses have been retained and have provided the rhythm which runs through the spaces. The original studs have been strengthened to improve the truss supports, and to allow substantial windows to be introduced. The trusses themselves have been kept but on the first floor have dictated the bedroom dividing walls. The height of the bottom truss member was such that the first floor corridor was built lower than the bedroom floor level to allow safe clearance. This gives a change of level to the ground floor ceiling over the shorter span running under the corridor, and helps to provide subsidiary spaces to the main one.

Materials have been kept to natural or stained timber, clay floor paviors, and similar country materials.

The fireplace is open on two sides, heating both dining and living areas.

The converted farm. On the left is house A, the low block house B and the house on the right house C.

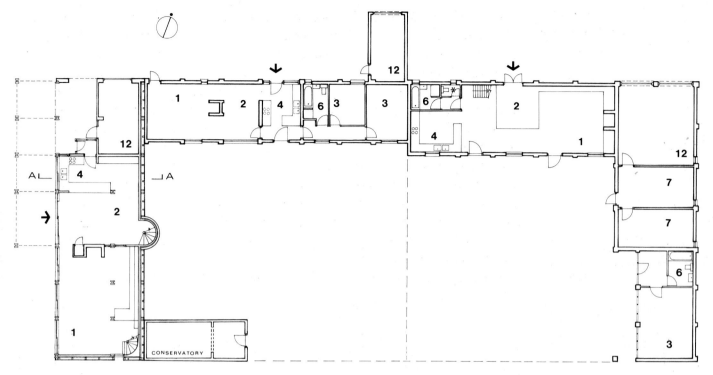

Ground floor plan showing houses A, B and C

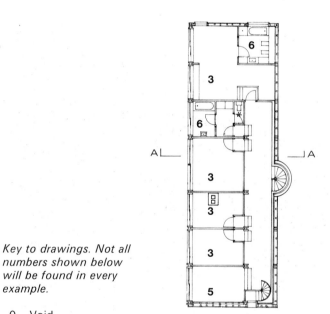

First floor plan of house A

0 5 10 15 F
0 1 2 3 4 M

House A, Section AA

Far right: The timber framework of the old farm has been kept and strengthened, and infill timber panels added. The owner added the boarding which was not as the architect intended.

Right: The interior of house A with a view of the stair brick 'drum' from the dining area.

Below: The study on the first floor of house A is glazed with obscured glass to screen the neighbouring building, but this adds a quality of diffused light.

**EXAMPLE 13
Terrace House,
Cambridge
Architect:
Keith Garbett**

This terrace house presents a reticent façade to the street, but has been thoroughly remodelled inside. The previous basement, largely underground, has been opened up vertically to the double height living space. Light now floods the old dark basement floor, and the bathroom is built against the roadside retaining wall. The ground floor has been cut half away to leave a living space gallery at pavement level. On the top floor, the ceiling has been removed and the height increased to provide a new ceiling under the pitched rafters.

The interior remodelling, although drastic, is detailed very simply. The handrails are a robust round section with a round substantial newel post, the various ceiling planes simply plastered, finishes plain and inexpensive. A stainless steel Pither stove dominates the living area.

The quiet elevation to the street belies the spacial games played within.

The small building at the rear has been designed to become a studio and garage, and, although shown on the drawings, has not yet been constructed.

The top floor study bedroom has a raised ceiling incorporating a rooflight which supplements the existing window to the street.

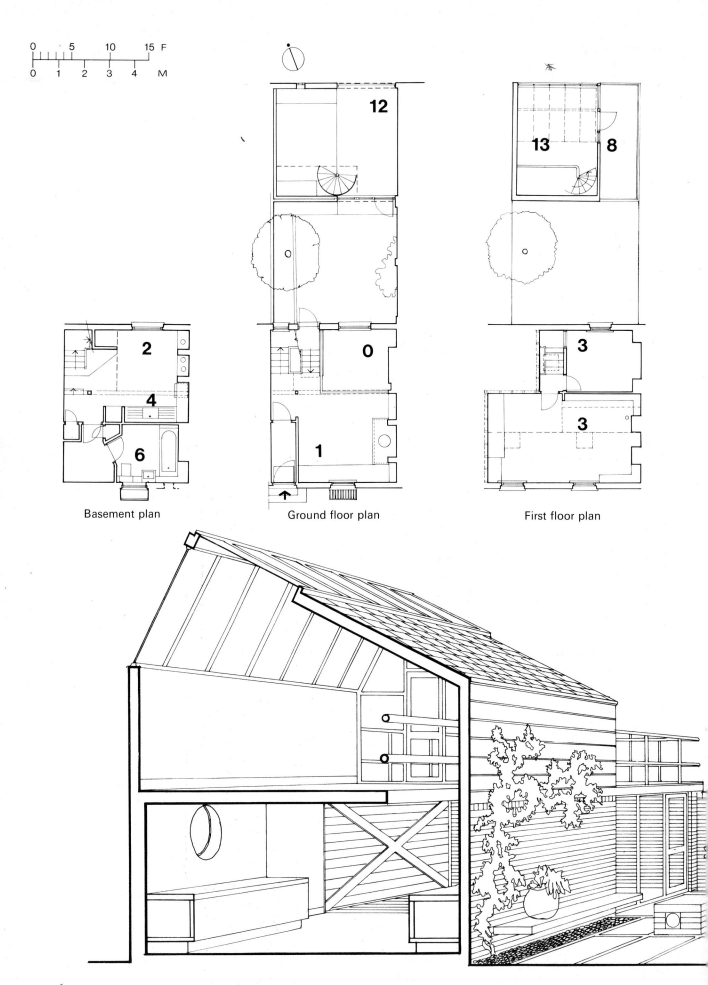

0 5 10 15 F

0 1 2 3 4 M

Basement plan   Ground floor plan   First floor plan

Key to drawings. Not all
numbers shown below
will be found in every
example.

0   Void
1   Living
2   Dining
3   Bedroom
4   Kitchen
5   Study
6   Bathroom
7   Store
8   Terrace
9   Gallery
10   Playroom
11   Laundry
12   Garage
13   Studio
14   Future extension or
     area for renewal
15   Conservatory
*   separate w.c.

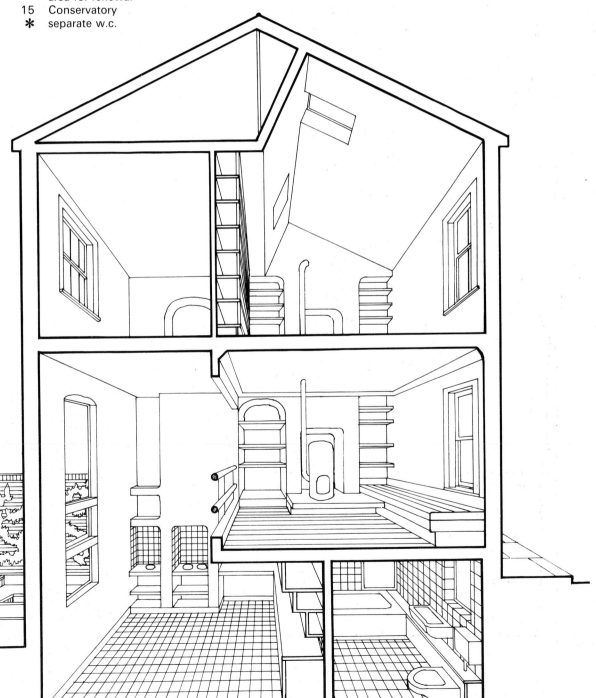

Right: The view from the stair landing at the garden level shows the double height over the kitchen, which is itself tucked out of sight from the living room.

Below: Looking from the living room across the void over the kitchen to the garden and studio.

The conversion of the upper floors of a large house such as this has possibilities over and above those of the lower floors. Fire escape requirements aside, the entry point to the upper flat can be the first and last door in the dwelling. The staircase will only be used by the occupant, unlike the main stair in the rest of the building, and thus can be opened up into the spaces on all floors allowing possibilities for manipulating the levels.

In this example, the owner required some special storage space. This was provided by raising the floor level over part of the main floor to allow storage below reached through access hatches in the new floor. This raised floor is reached up a short flight of steps and itself leads to a short bridging staircase on the diagonal for access to the small bedroom and terrace.

The existing double roof with central valley gutter was removed and replaced with a new flat roof with mansard, rooflight and small terrace. By using a flat roof an extra bedroom could be fitted in at the higher level and a specially high ceiling gained for the main living area.

The living room looking towards the raised storage area, with the bedroom mezzanine on the left, over the main entrance staircase.

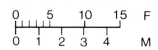

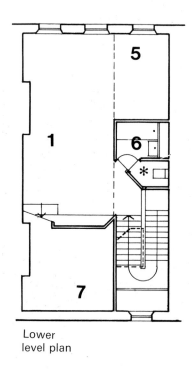

Lower level plan

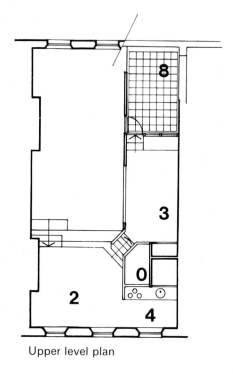

Upper level plan

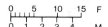

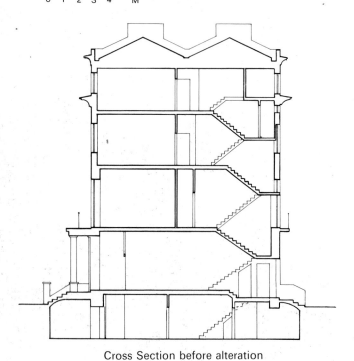

Cross Section before alteration

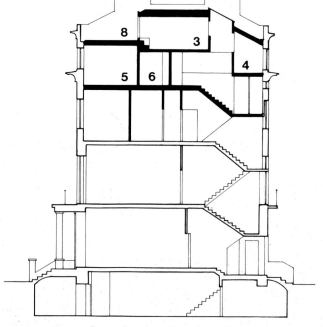

Cross Section after alteration
Floors altered shown solid

Right: The terrace seen from the mezannine bedroom.

Below: Looking up the short diagonal flight of stairs to the bedroom mezzanine.

Below right: The view from the mezzanine down to the living room level.

EXAMPLE 15
House Extension,
Buckinghamshire
Architect:
Aldington and Craig

The existing house on the site, basically a turn-of-the-century worker's cottage, has been altered to provide a larger kitchen and bathroom. The main part of this contract however is the long brick and timber extension built against an old garden wall. It forms a sheltered corner against the existing house and provides a living room with dining space enclosed partly within a brick 'drum'. Beyond the living room is a studio with upper floor enclosed in a monopitch roof finished with plain tiles. Both levels of the studio have walls lined with spruce.

The living and dining spaces are fully double-glazed with fixed and sliding

full height windows on the south side, giving views across the bosky garden to the Chiltern Hills beyond.

The new extension is connected to the house by a glazed link which also provides access to the rear garden. This method of adding a modern extension enables a different architecture to be deployed in new work without a clash with the existing house. It also of course makes an umbilical connection with the parent building which involves the minimum alteration to the existing structure. Heating, apart from the open fire, is by two large fan-assisted electric storage heaters.

View of the extension from the garden. The original house is on the right.

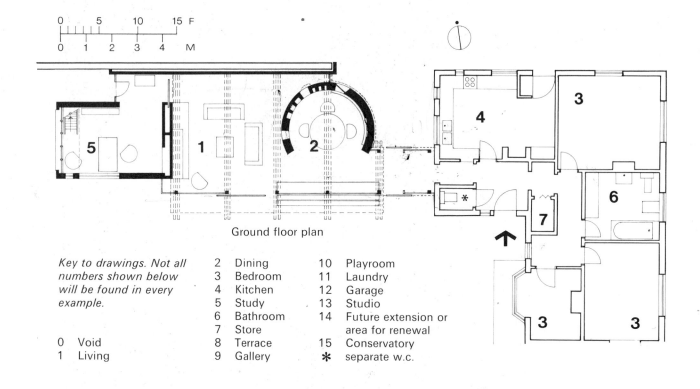

Ground floor plan

Key to drawings. Not all
numbers shown below
will be found in every
example.

0	Void	2 Dining	10 Playroom
1	Living	3 Bedroom	11 Laundry
		4 Kitchen	12 Garage
		5 Study	13 Studio
		6 Bathroom	14 Future extension or
		7 Store	area for renewal
		8 Terrace	15 Conservatory
		9 Gallery	✳ separate w.c.

The small garden court
showing the link to the
original house and the
'drum' of the dining room.

Right: There is a studio at first floor level at the end of the extension.

Below: The interior of the new building. The dining room is on the right.

EXAMPLE 16
Mitchells Close,
Haddington, Scotland
Architect:
Campbell & Arnott

Commissioned by The East Lothian County Council and supported by Grant Aid from the Historic Buildings council, this urban renewal scheme for a small close off Market Street has restored some of the old uses to the buildings that had become derelict. The aim was to recreate the mixed workshop and living accommodation that gave the original life to the close. There is now a shop, plumber's workshop and office, hand loom weaver's workshop, leather craftsman's workshop, two maisonettes and one attic flat, with a clinic in a new building.

Roofs and floors were removed, outside walls repaired and roofs rebuilt to the old ridge time. The buildings were made as near the original as possible but some new and old materials were mixed to get the final result.

The scheme shows the regeneration of a small urban 'backwater' possessing strong regional characteristics and bringing it back into the life of the town.

The Close before renewal.

Right: An interior of one of the flats on the top floor. The room has been opened up to the roof ridge to obtain more height on what might otherwise be a cramped floor.

Below: After renewal. As well as flats in the four storey buildings, the lower buildings now include a plumbers, woollen shop and studio. The buildings at the end of the Close over the archway were not part of this contract.

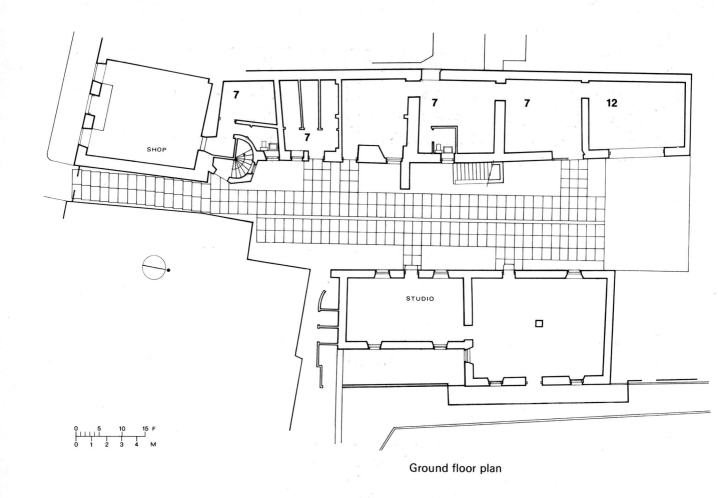

SHOP

7

7

7

7

12

STUDIO

0   5   10   15 F
0   1   2   3   4   M

Ground floor plan

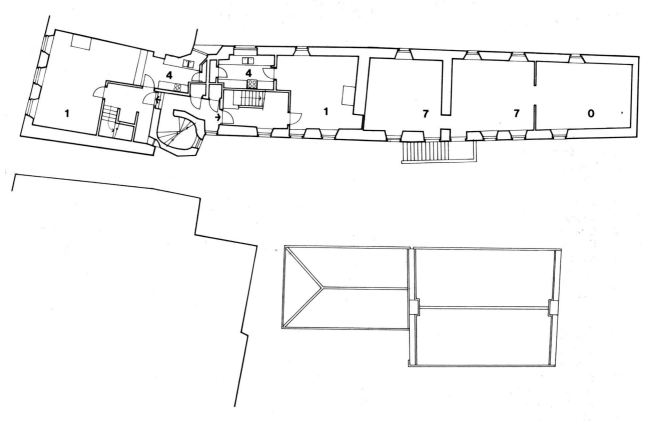

1

4

4

1

7

7

0

First floor plan

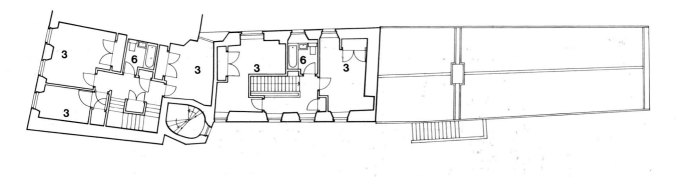

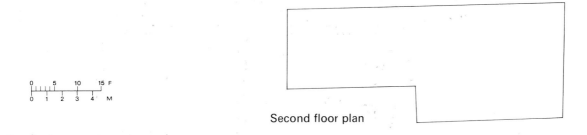

0 5 10 15 F
0 1 2 3 4 M

Second floor plan

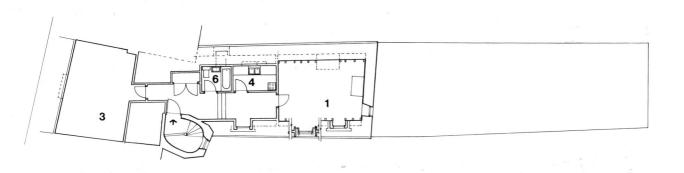

Third floor plan

Key to drawings. Not all
numbers shown below
will be found in every
example.

0   Void
1   Living
2   Dining
3   Bedroom
4   Kitchen
5   Study
6   Bathroom
7   Store
8   Terrace
9   Gallery
10 Playroom
11 Laundry
12 Garage
13 Studio
14 Future extension or
    area for renewal
15 Conservatory
*   separate w.c.

**EXAMPLE 17
Cottage,
Over Alderley,
Cheshire
Architect: Hayes
Turner & Partners**

Built about 1900 'in the style of a branch railway station' as the architect describes it, the exterior has been basically retained and the interior re-planned. The new extension consists of a brick box with pyramid roof, joined by a glass link to the old building.

The outbuildings have been simply adapted for use as a car port, sun bathing roof and garage, and provide a foil to the main house. Internally, the planning is devised to be flexible using a series of inter-communicating spaces which also allow the magnificent views outward to be experienced.

Finishes are extremely basic, consisting of the old external brick, now partly internal, and rough plaster. Roller Blinds, the same colour as the walls, are used over the windows. Floors are of timber, stone flags, carpets and rugs.

The entrance hall with study beyond. Stone paving runs through from outside into the hall and kitchen.

The living room on the ground floor with sunken sitting area.

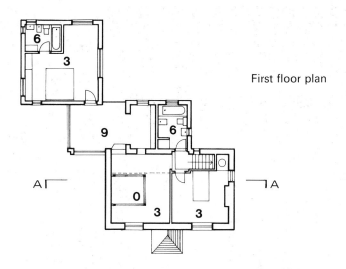

First floor plan

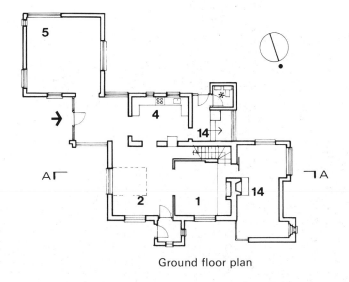

Ground floor plan

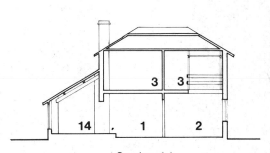

Section AA

Key to drawings. Not all numbers shown below will be found in every example.

0	Void	2	Dining
1	Living	3	Bedroom
		4	Kitchen
		5	Study
		6	Bathroom
		7	Store
		8	Terrace
		9	Gallery

10	Playroom
11	Laundry
12	Garage
13	Studio
14	Future extension or area for renewal
15	Conservatory
*	separate w.c.

Above: View from the first
floor bedroom diagonally
through the void over the
dining space. There is a bed
raised to the ceiling level
which can be lowered to the
balustrade to complete the
bedroom.

Right: The original house is
on the right. The left hand
building and two-storey
entrance have been added.

EXAMPLE 18
Converted Granary,
Blakeney, Norfolk
Architects:
Fielden and Mawson

The scheme includes five flats and two shops. The original granary was used as a warehouse for shipping until the harbour silted up.

Built about 1750, this granary was originally a warehouse used by shipping before the harbour silted up. The project was the conversion of this building into shops and flats. Two shops were incorporated at ground level and five flats on one, two and three levels in the remainder.

The walls are unusual in that they are brick faced outside, but flint inside, contrary to local tradition. The roof is finished with local red pantile.

The architects have designed the conversion in a straight early-industrial manner with sea-side overtones. The design of the shop windows, rather like show cases, might seem a little 'twee' for such a robust architecture but does successfully differentiate between shop and other windows in the building.

Inside, the staircases are pine-boarded, with pine handrails. Rafters and trusses are left exposed inside, with insulation sheet material applied over the rafters and under the tiles.

164

Right: The converted granary with its 'functional tradition' outside staircases and generally robust detailing.

Below: Interior showing pine staircase with upper level gallery in one of the flats.

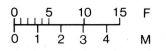

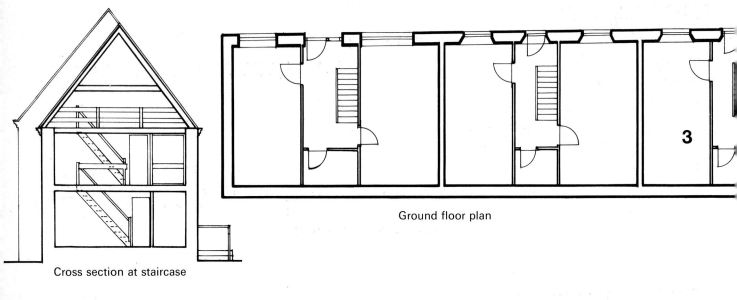

Cross section at staircase

Ground floor plan

```
0    5    10   15   F
|--|--|--|--|--|--|--|
0   1   2   3   4    M
```

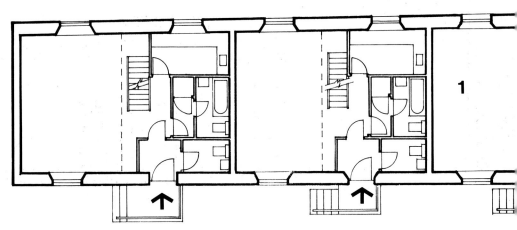

First floor plan

Key to drawings. Not all
numbers shown below
will be found in every
example.

0   Void
1   Living
2   Dining
3   Bedroom
4   Kitchen
5   Study
6   Bathroom
7   Store
8   Terrace
9   Gallery
10 Playroom
11 Laundry
12 Garage
13 Studio
14 Future extension or
    area for renewal
15 Conservatory
*   separate w.c.

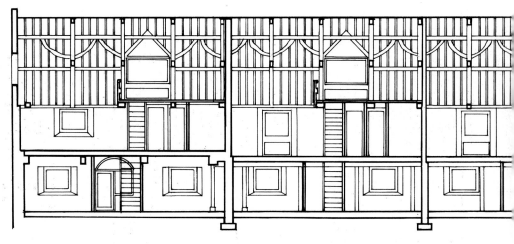

Long section

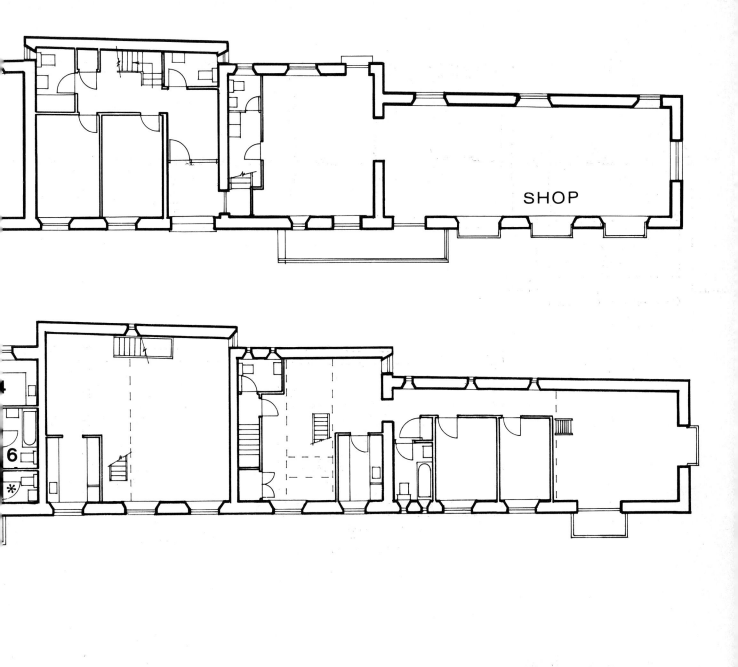

SHOP

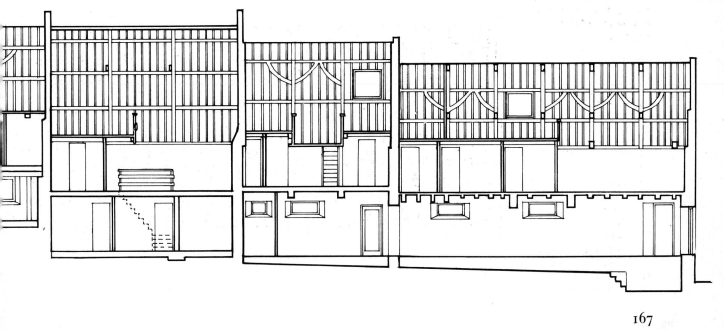

EXAMPLE 19
Studio Conversion,
Hampstead, London
Architect:
John Moore

The original building was a purpose built studio with north light, gallery, and separate kitchen.

The architect has enlarged the whole complex which now comprises bedrooms, a new kitchen-dining room and entrance hall. The gallery in the large high studio has been dismantled and a new one constructed at the opposite end which provides the main bedroom, and is reached by a spiral staircase. Below the gallery, the floor has been sunk down to give a snug sitting area round the solid fuel stove.

Key to drawings. Not all numbers shown below will be found in every example.

0 Void
1 Living
2 Dining
3 Bedroom
4 Kitchen
5 Study
6 Bathroom
7 Store
8 Terrace
9 Gallery
10 Playroom
11 Laundry
12 Garage
13 Studio
14 Future extension or area for renewal
15 Conservatory
* separate w.c.

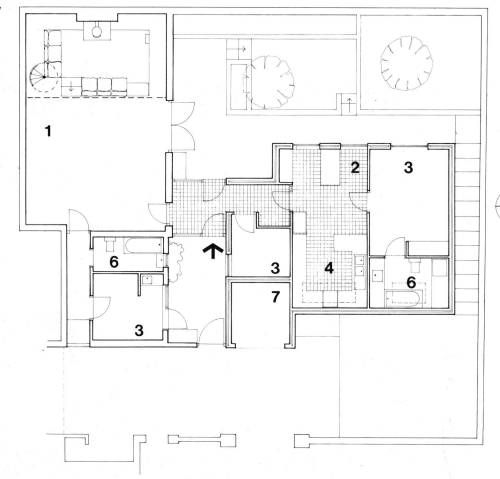

Ground floor plan

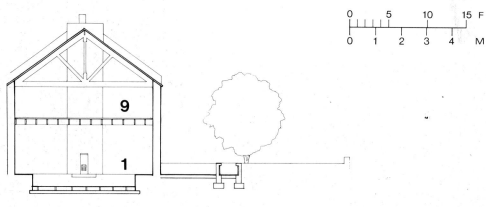

0   5   10   15 F
0 1 2 3 4 M

Cross Section through sitting area and gallery

168

The kitchen in the new extension is lit mainly from above but has views out to the garden through the associated dining space.

The fine roof trusses dominate the studio. The extensions have been designed very sympathetically and are low and cozy and in contrast to the large studio space. Provision has been made for the addition of another floor over the bedroom and kitchen wing in the future. The entrance to the enlarged house is played down. A simple small scale courtyard leads to the front door set in a low link between studio and kitchen. Moving from the low entrance into the large volume of the studio is a pleasant experience.

Above: The main entrance forms a link between the old studio on the left and the new extension on the right.

Right: The old studio has been altered to incorporate a sleeping gallery, with a sunken sitting area below it providing an element of cosiness, in what is otherwise a very large space.

**EXAMPLE 20
Converted Granary,
Driffield, Yorkshire
Architects:
MacCormac &
Jamieson**

This granary has been converted into flats for a private developer. The magnificent early industrial building was well suited to the planning of small flats between 16 and 20 ft (4.87 and 6.09 m) apart. On the ground floor the flats are on one level; on the upper floors maisonette flats have been incorporated, most being reached from access galleries. There are some variations to these to take account of special parts of the building where there are irregularities in the plan. Being listed as a building of historic interest, the external detailing has been kept in character. On the street side, two new staircase enclosures have been constructed in the same form as the original cantilevered hoists, with weatherboarding and canopies. On the canal side, balconies have been built out in timber, the detail copied from a windmill of the same period.

Some windows have been slightly altered to gain compliance with daylighting bye-laws. New dormer windows have been added, old loading doors reconstructed with vertical boarding. French windows, in the form of stable doors, were added to the ground floor flats where additional daylight was needed.

Part of the converted building from across the canal.

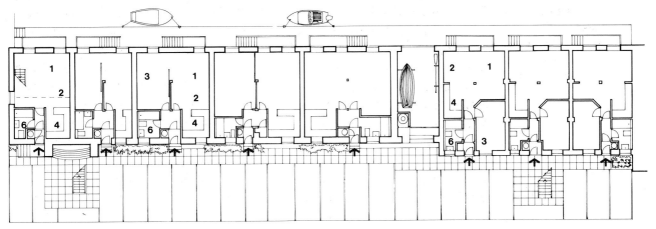

Ground floor plan

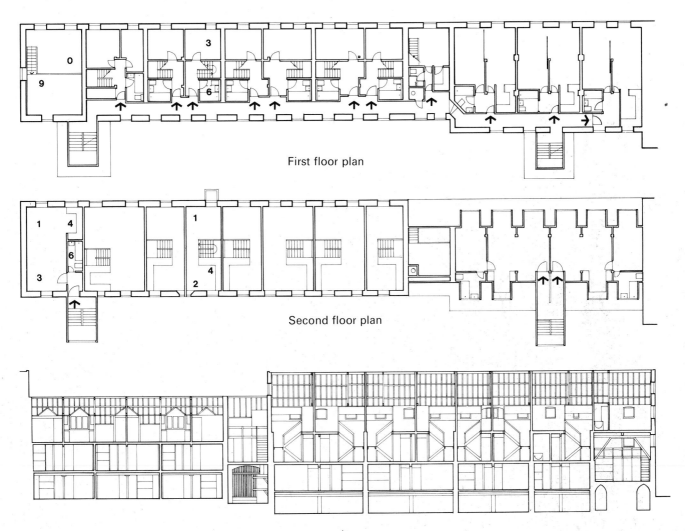

First floor plan

Second floor plan

Long section

Key to drawings. Not all
numbers shown below
will be found in every
example.

	2 Dining	10	Playroom
	3 Bedroom	11	Laundry
	4 Kitchen	12	Garage
	5 Study	13	Studio
	6 Bathroom	14	Future extension or
	7 Store		area for renewal
0 Void	8 Terrace	15	Conservatory
1 Living	9 Gallery	∗	separate w.c.

173

Right: The canal side elevation with balconies derived from windmill detailing.

Far right: The two white boarded stair towers to the upper level gallery continue the early industrial functional tradition on the road elevation.

Below right: Interior of a top floor unit before furnishing.

Below: The robust details of the old granary have been followed in spirit in the new elements.

EXAMPLE 21
Houses, London Borough of Camden
Architect: Castle Park Dean & Hook

There is a large estate in The Kentish Town area of London consisting of about 100 large early Victorian family houses. These were bought by the local authority in the late 1950s and contained sitting tenants. The Council's policy is to modernise the properties over a period of years to allow the inhabitants of the estates to move to modernised houses as they are converted. They are being converted by the architects at a rate of about 12 per year to full Parker Morris standards, including central heating, and attract the full grants available. Contracts are let in groups of two or four houses. At the same time, the forecourts of the houses are being redesigned.

In common with other conversion work done by this firm, these houses are altered with the aid of a computerised processing system in the production of specifications. Much of the building work to convert houses is repetitive from one house to the next (there are 100 to be done on this estate in this example) and, once codified, the information can be tabulated and punched onto tape, to be recalled and assembled to cover a particular job.

The architect can thus 'write' the specification for the job on site by phrase selection as he visits each part of the house. This is then assembled, checked, standard clauses on Preliminaries and Materials and Workmanship added and the whole specification printed out: the whole being produced in approximately one week. A conventional, typed, specification would be likely to take three weeks from start to finish.

The architects state that this shortened pre-contract period benefits the client as the contractor can be got on site sooner, the building is empty for less time and deterioration of it is reduced.

Time can be saved as drawings are simplified and become location and reference documents only, stripped of specification notes but containing clause reference numbers. The initial setting up of the computer information would be expensive but the costs defrayed to the point of profitability within a reasonable time.

The stolid Victorian semi-detached houses after renewal. The old trees in front of this particular house have been pruned and incorporated in the land-scaping of the fore-court.

owing kitchen
oor to garden,
h side louvres.

The reorganised fore-court incorporates a dustbin enclosure as well as paving and cobbles.

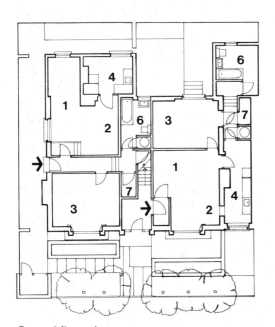

Ground floor plan

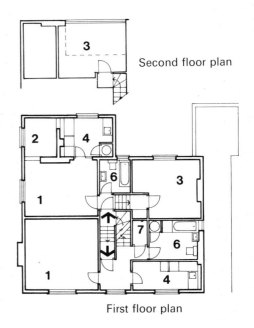

Second floor plan

First floor plan

Key to drawings. Not all numbers shown below will be found in every example.

0	Void	8	Terrace
1	Living	9	Gallery
2	Dining	10	Playroom
3	Bedroom	11	Laundry
4	Kitchen	12	Garage
5	Study	13	Studio
6	Bathroom	14	Future extension or area for renewal
7	Store	15	Conservatory
		*	separate w.c.

EXAMPLE 22
'Black Road,
Macclesfield
Architect:
Rod Hackney and
Associates

This scheme is of interest not only for the design of the improvements but for the way it was organised.

The Black Road area was scheduled for clearance by the local authority. The 160 year-old buildings were textile workers' houses in a very sorry state. The residents formed themselves into an action group and mounted a campaign and eventually got their houses declared a General Improvement Area, calling themselves the Black Road Area Residents Association. Having saved their houses in the short term, they persuaded the Council to give grants and other assistance to their project. Rod Hackney lived in one of the houses and agreed to convert his house as a 'show house' and as a prototype. One of the great points of interest, however, in this project is that the residents themselves did much of the actual work. Contractors were brought in to do specialist jobs but the prototype house was also used to gain experience in building for the residents, to train them for the renovation of the other houses. Some helped on houses other than their own. Individual houses have their own variations to suit their owners although the outside appearance of each house is not very varied, the general proportions of doors and windows being maintained. Externally, the surroundings have been improved and landscaped, and some parking provided. From having been opposed to the scheme initially, the local authority were impressed with the strength of purpose of the residents and cooperated in many ways to allow the area to be renovated by the residents and their contractors.

Black Road housing before renewal.

In assessing the lessons to be learnt, Rod Hackney considers that the following points are important:

1 The presence of a qualified person living within the improvement area was of great value in negotiating with the Council and contractors

2 The rectangular 'island' site proved ideal, with its inside and outside spaces, for a successful environmental scheme

3 By concentrating on a small compact area and making sure that all the houses were improved, the Group were able to ensure that their houses, being within self-contained boundaries, would not prejudice future plans for surrounding neighbourhoods. The scheme would have failed if a large pilot scheme had been chosen and only random house improvements carried out

4 The Group emphasised their attitude of cooperation with the Council and avoided criticism of individuals within the local authority. This in turn ensured positive cooperation from them

5 The scheme was carried out as fast as possible to maintain enthusiasm and prevent the residents losing interest

Rod Hackney gave a paper to a conference at the Civic Centre, Newcastle-upon-Tyne, organised by the Royal Society of Health. This description is derived in part from that paper.

Smith's Terrace after renewal.

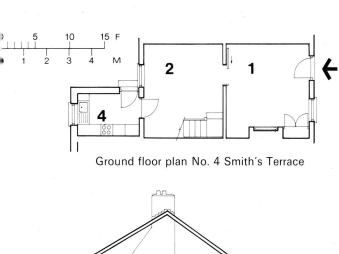

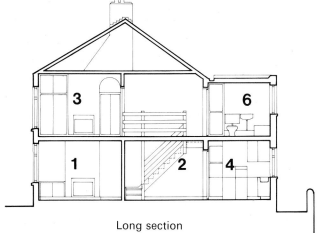

Ground floor plan No. 4 Smith's Terrace

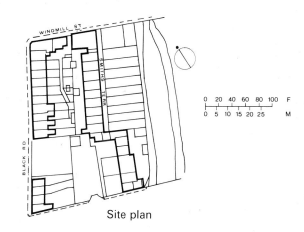

First floor plan No. 4 Smith's Terrace

Long section

Site plan

Right: The interior of the scheme has been extensively landscaped.

Below: Interiors of this self-help scheme have been reorganised very simply, in order to accommodate every taste, with a new kitchen and bathroom extension added in this case, at Smith's Terrace.

Bibliography

A. J. LEGAL HANDBOOK. Evelyn Freeth & Peter Davey. Architectural Press Ltd.

A. J. METRIC GUIDE to the BUILDING REGULATIONS. A. J. Elder. Architectural Press Ltd.

A. J. METRIC HANDBOOK. Jan Sliwa, Leslie Fairweather. Architectural Press Ltd.

BUILDING REGULATIONS EXPLAINED and ILLUSTRATED. Whyte & Powell-Smith. Crosby Lockwood.

BUILDING RESEARCH ESTABLISHMENT DIGESTS (general topics). H.M.S.O.

CARE OF OLD BUILDINGS TODAY, The. Donald Insall. Architectural Press Ltd.

CODE OF PRACTICE. Means of Escape in Case of Fire. G.L.C.

CODE OF PRACTICE. CP3 Chapter 4 Pt 1. British Standard Institution.

COMMON FURNITURE BEETLE, The. Technical Note 47. Building Research Establishment.

DAMAGE BY AMBROSIA (pinhole borer) BEETLES. Technical note 55. Building Research Establishment

DEATH-WATCH BEETLE, The. Technical note 45. Building Research Establishment.

DECAY IN BUILDINGS. Technical note 44. Building Research Establishment.

DICTIONARY OF BUILDING. John S. Scott. Penguin Books Ltd.

EXTENDING YOUR HOUSE. Ian Morris. Consumers Association.

GUIDE TO THE LONDON BUILDING (CONSTRUCTIONAL) BYELAWS 1972. Pitt & Dufton. Architectural Press Ltd.

GUIDE TO DOMESTIC BUILDING SURVEYS. Jack Bowyer. Architectural Press Ltd.

HOUSE BOOK, The. Terence Conran. Mitchell Beazley.

HOUSE IMPROVEMENT AND CONVERSION. DOE Welsh Office. H.M.S.O.

HOUSE LONGHORN BEETLE, The. Technical note 39. Building Research Establishment.

OLD HOUSES, NEW INTERIORS. Jacques Debaigts. Barrie & Jenkins.

OUTLINE OF PLANNING LAW. Desmond Heap. Sweet & Maxwell.

PARTY STRUCTURE RIGHTS IN LONDON. W. A. Leach. Estates Gazette Ltd.

PATTERN OF ENGLISH BUILDING, The. Alec Clifton-Taylor. Faber.

PRINCIPLES AND PRACTICE OF TOWN & COUNTRY PLANNING. Lewis Keeble. Estates Gazette Ltd.

RIGHT TO LIGHT, The. Brian Anstey and Michael Chavasse. Estates Gazette Ltd.

SLUM CLEARANCE AND IMPROVEMENTS. Scottish Development Dept. H.M.S.O.

SOUND INSULATION IN BUILDINGS. Humphreys & Melluish. H.M.S.O.

SPECIFICATION VOLS. 1 & 2. Dex Harrison. Architectural Press Ltd.

SPECIFICATION WRITING FOR ARCHITECTS & SURVEYORS. A & C Willis. Crosby Lockwood.

SUMMARY OF TOWN & COUNTRY PLANNING LAW. A. J. Lomnicki. Batsford.

THERMAL INSULATION OF BUILDINGS. Handisyde & Melluish. H.M.S.O.

TOWN & COUNTRY PLANNING IN BRITAIN. J. B. Cullingworth. Allen and Unwin.

YOUR HOUSE—THE OUTSIDE VIEW. John Prizeman. Hutchinson.

Index